Best of Fons&Porter

scrap EXPLOSION
QUILTS

LEISURE ARTS
the art of everyday living
www.leisurearts.com

FONS & PORTER STAFF
Editors-in-Chief Marianne Fons and Liz Porter

Editor Jean Nolte
Managing Editor Debra Finan
Associate Editor Diane Tomlinson
Technical Writer Kristine Peterson

Art Director Tony Jacobson

Interactive Editor Morgan Abel
Sewing Specialists Cindy Hathaway, Colleen Tauke
Contributing Photographers Dean Tanner, Kathryn Gamble, Craig Anderson
Contributing Photo Assistants Mary Mouw, DeElda Wittmack

Publisher Kristi Loeffelholz
Advertising Manager Cristy Adamski
Retail Manager Sharon Hart
Web Site Manager Phillip Zacharias
Fons & Porter Staff Shelle Goodwin, Sheyenne Manning, Anne Welker, Karla Wesselmann, Kelsey Wolfswinkel

New Track Media LLC
President and CEO Stephen J. Kent
Chief Financial Officer Mark F. Arnett
President, Book Publishing W. Budge Wallis
Vice President/Group Publisher Tina Battock
Vice President, Circulation Nicole McGuire
Vice President, Production Barbara Schmitz
Production Manager Dominic M. Taormina
IT Manager Denise Donnarumma
Renewal and Billing Manager Nekeya Dancy
Online Subscriptions Manager Jodi Lee

Our Mission Statement
Our goal is for you to enjoy making quilts as much as we do.

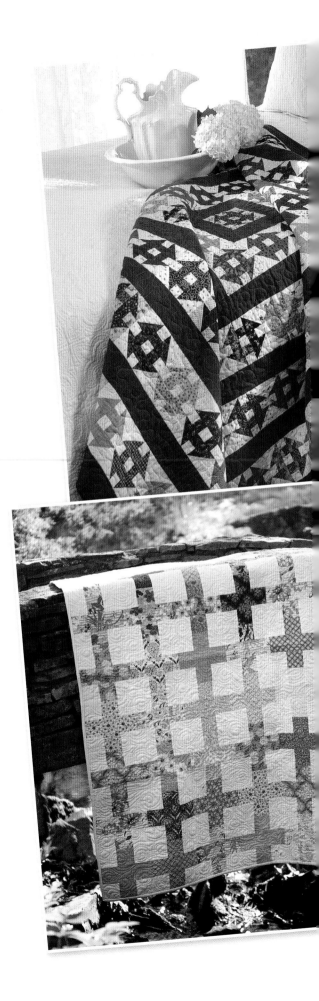

LEISURE ARTS STAFF
Vice President of Editorial Susan White Sullivan
Creative Art Director Katherine Laughlin
Publications Director Leah Lampirez
Special Projects Director Susan Frantz Wiles
Prepress Technician Stephanie Johnson

President and Chief Executive Officer Rick Barton
Senior Vice President of Operations Jim Dittrich
Vice President of Finance Fred F. Pruss
Vice President of Sales-Retail Books Martha Adams
Vice President of Mass Market Bob Bewighouse
Vice President of Technology and Planning Laticia Mull Dittrich
Controller Tiffany P. Childers
Information Technology Director Brian Roden
Director of E-Commerce Mark Hawkins
Manager of E-Commerce Robert Young
Retail Customer Service Manager Stan Raynor

Library of Congress Control Number: 2013957628
ISBN-13/EAN: 978-1-4647-0871-8
UPC: 0-28906-06058-4

We're thrilled to bring you this collection of some of our very favorite scrap quilts! The projects we've included are among our most popular of all time. You'll find challenging as well as easy patchwork, plus dashes of lovely appliqué. Enjoy the beautiful photography as you browse through the pages to find the quilt that's just right for you. Whether you are a batik-lover, a traditionalist, or a fan of contemporary fabric choices, you'll find plenty to love. You'll also appreciate our trademarked Sew Easy lessons that will guide you via step-by-step photographs through any project-specific special techniques. So go to your stash (or your local quilt shop), gather up some fabrics, and start stitching!

Happy quilting,

Marianne & Liz

20

Sparkle Punch	6
Floral Explosion	10
Color Play	14
String Star	20
Hello, Garden	28
Triple Four Patch	32
Petals	36
Feedsack Flowers	42
Friendship Rings	48
Around and Around	54
Barbed Wire	60
Scrappy Stars	64
Scrappy Triangles	70
Texas Two Step	74
Scrapbook	80
Tossed Greens	84
Simply Squares	88
1930s Re-Bloom	92
Tangerine Zoo	96

102

88

Zig and Zag   102

Pixie Sticks   106

Traffic Jam   112

Scrap Box Diamonds   118

Monkey Business   122

Dash Around the Square   126

Techniques

Sew Easy: Cutting 60° Diamonds
    and Pyramids   27

Sew Easy: Log Cabin Hexagons   47

Sew Easy: Fusible Web Appliqué   59

Sew Easy: Quick Triangle-Squares   79

Sew Easy: Needle-Turn Appliqué   95

Sew Easy: Crazy-Pieced Blocks   111

Sew Easy: Mitered Borders   117

Sew Easy: String Piecing   121

General Instructions   132

48

42

122

Sparkle Punch

This quilt is fun to make—you'll put your design wall to good use. The wonkiness of the star points and variety of prints really make the stars sparkle. Designer Elizabeth Hartman says, "It's my interpretation of the interlocking-star trend."

PROJECT RATING: INTERMEDIATE

Size: 60" × 72"

MATERIALS

20 fat quarters★ assorted prints in pink, teal, black, gray, purple, and brown for stars

3¾ yard gray solid for background

⅝ yard brown print for binding

4 yards backing fabric

Twin-size quilt batting

★fat quarter = 18" × 20"

Cutting

Measurements include ¼" seam allowances.

From fat quarters, cut a total of:

• 80 sets of 5 (3½") squares. Set aside 1 square of each set to be used for star centers. Cut remaining squares in half diagonally to make 80 sets of 8 half-square triangles *(Whole Star Diagram).*

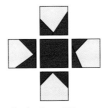

Whole Star Diagram

• 14 sets of 4 (3½") squares. Set aside 1 square of each set to be used for star centers. Cut remaining squares in half diagonally to make 14 sets of 6 half-square triangles *(Three-Quarter Star Diagram).*

Three-Quarter Star Diagram

• 2 sets of 3 (3½") squares. Set aside 1 square of each set to be used for star centers. Cut remaining squares in half diagonally to make 2 sets of 4 half-square triangles *(Half Star Diagram).*

Half Star Diagram

• 18 single (3½") squares. Cut squares in half diagonally to make 18 sets of 2 half-square triangles *(Quarter Star Diagram).*

Quarter Star Diagram

NOTE: The partial stars will be around the edges of the quilt, so make sure they're not all the same fabric or color.

From gray solid, cut:

• 35 (3½"-wide) strips. From strips, cut 384 (3½") squares.

From brown print, cut:

• 8 (2¼"-wide) strips for binding.

Star Point Assembly

1. Referring to *Star Point Unit Diagrams*, place 1 print triangle atop 1 gray square, right sides facing. Stitch with a ¼" seam allowance across corner. Press open to reveal triangle. Trim gray square ¼" beyond stitching. Repeat for adjacent corner using a matching triangle.

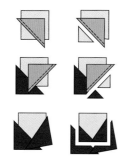

Star Point Unit Diagrams

Sew **Smart**™

The star points are wonky. Place print triangles on gray squares at varying angles. Just be sure that when triangle is pressed open, it covers corner of gray square underneath. Then trim corner of gray square. —Elizabeth

2. Trim square to 3½" to complete 1 Star Point Unit. Make 384 Star Point Units.

Quilt Assembly

1. Lay out Star Point Units and star center squares as shown in *Quilt Top Assembly Diagram*.

2. Join into sections; join sections to complete quilt top.

Sew **Smart**™

I like to start arranging star components near the center and work my way out to the sides. The partial stars will all end up around the edges of the quilt top.

—Elizabeth

Finishing

1. Divide backing into 2 (2-yard) lengths. Join panels lengthwise. Seam will run horizontally.

2. Layer backing, batting, and quilt top; baste. Quilt as desired. Quilt shown was quilted with an allover zigzag design (*Quilting Diagram*).

3. Join 2¼"-wide brown print strips into 1 continuous piece for straight-grain French-fold binding. Add binding to quilt.

Quilt Top Assembly Diagram

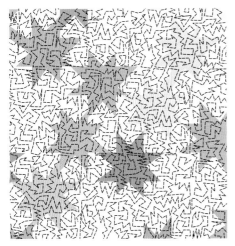

Quilting Diagram

TRIED & TRUE

This technique is fun to do with any style of fabrics. We used reproduction prints from the Alexandria collection by Jo Morton for Andover Fabrics.

DESIGNER

Elizabeth Hartman is a self-taught quilter from Portland, Oregon. She is the author of the popular blog ohfransson. com, and *The Practical Guide to Patchwork*, which was the winner of the Next Generation Indie Book Award for Best How-To Book of 2011. Her second book, *Modern Patchwork* was published in May 2012.

QUILT BY **Amanda Murphy**.
MACHINE QUILTED BY **Deborah Norris**.

Floral Explosion

This quilt is great for using your scraps, coordinated or not. We like it in the juicy colors designer Amanda Murphy chose from her Veranda collection. Make four extra blocks for the coordinating pillow.

PROJECT RATING: INTERMEDIATE

Size: 84" × 92¼"

Blocks: 72 (8¼") blocks

MATERIALS

NOTE: Fabrics in the quilt shown are from the Veranda collection by Amanda Murphy for Robert Kaufman Fabrics.

1¼ yards dark pink print for border

2¾ yards blue print for blocks and border

1 yard green stripe for border

½ yard dark orange print for blocks and border

¾ yard white solid for border

¾ yard each of 10 assorted prints in orange, green, blue, and pink for blocks

7⅞ yards backing fabric

Queen-size quilt batting

Cutting

Measurements include ¼" seam allowances.

From dark pink print, cut:

- 10 (1½"-wide) strips. Piece strips to make 2 (1½" × 96") side border strips and 2 (1½" × 88") top and bottom border strips.
- 2 (4"-wide) strips. From strips, cut 18 (4") squares. Cut squares in half diagonally in both directions to make 72 quarter-square B triangles.
- 4 (3⅝"-wide) strips. From strips, cut 36 (3⅝") squares. Cut squares in half diagonally to make 72 half-square A triangles.

From blue print, cut:

- 10 (5"-wide) strips. Piece strips to make 2 (5" × 96") side border strips and 2 (5" × 88") top and bottom border strips.
- 2 (4"-wide) strips. From strips, cut 18 (4") squares. Cut squares in half diagonally in both directions to make 72 quarter-square B triangles.

- 4 (3⅝"-wide) strips. From strips, cut 36 (3⅝") squares. Cut squares in half diagonally to make 72 half-square A triangles.
- 10 (2¼"-wide) strips for binding.

From green stripe, cut:

- 10 (2½"-wide) strips. Piece strips to make 2 (2½" × 96") side border strips and 2 (2½" × 88") top and bottom border strips.

From dark orange print , cut:

- 12 (1¼"-wide) strips. From strips, cut 360 (1¼") C squares.

From white solid, cut:

- 9 (2"-wide) strips. From strips, cut 34 (2" × 8¾") D rectangles and 4 (2") E squares.

From each assorted print, cut:

- 2 (4"-wide) strips. From strips, cut 18 (4") squares. Cut squares in half diagonally in both directions to make 72 quarter-square B triangles.
- 4 (3⅝"-wide) strips. From strips, cut 36 (3⅝") squares. Cut squares in half diagonally to make 72 half-square A triangles.

Block Assembly

1. Choose 2 sets of 4 matching A triangles and 1 set of 4 matching A triangles and 12 B triangles.

2. Join 1 A triangle and 2 B triangles as shown in *Flying Geese Unit Diagrams*. Make 2 sets of 2 matching Flying Geese Units.

Flying Geese Unit Diagrams

3. Join 4 A triangles as shown in *Hourglass Unit Diagrams* to make 1 Hourglass Unit.

Hourglass Unit Diagrams

4. Lay out Hourglass Unit, Flying Geese Units, and remaining A and B triangles as shown in *Block Assembly Diagrams*. Join into diagonal rows; join rows.

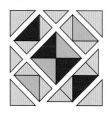 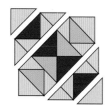

Block Assembly Diagrams

5. Place 1 dark orange print C square atop pieced block, right sides facing. Stitch diagonally from corner to corner as shown. Trim ¼" beyond stitching. Press open to reveal triangle. Repeat for remaining corners to complete 1 block *(Block Diagram)*. Make 72 blocks.

Block Diagram

Inner Border Assembly

1. Referring to *Border Unit Diagrams*, place 1 dark orange print C square atop 1 white D rectangle, right sides facing. Stitch diagonally from corner to corner as shown. Trim ¼" beyond stitching. Press open to reveal triangle. Repeat for adjacent corner to complete 1 Border Unit. Make 34 Border Units.

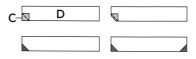

Border Unit Diagrams

2. In the same manner, make 4 Border Corners using 1 dark orange print C square and 1 white E square in each *(Border Corner Diagram)*.

Border Corner Diagram

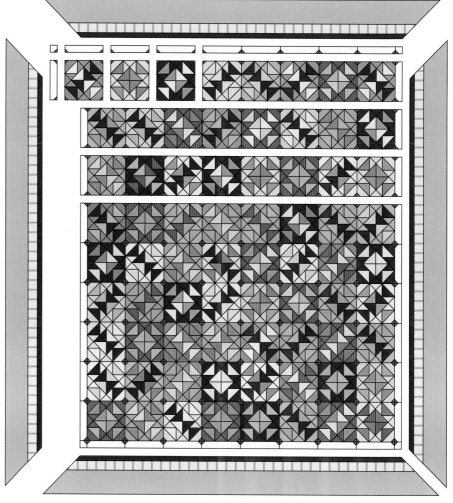

Quilt Top Assembly Diagram

Quilt Assembly

1. Lay out blocks, Border Units, and Border Corners as shown in *Quilt Top Assembly Diagram*.
2. Join into rows; join rows to complete quilt center.
3. Join 1 dark pink print side border strip, 1 green stripe side border strip, and 1 blue print side border strip to make 1 side outer border. Make 2 side outer borders.
4. In the same manner, make 2 top and bottom outer borders.
5. Add outer borders to quilt, mitering corners.

> ## Web **Extra**
> **For instructions on mitering borders, visit our Web site at: FonsandPorter.com/mborders.**

Finishing

1. Divide backing into 3 (2⅝-yard) lengths. Join panels lengthwise. Seams will run horizontally.
2. Layer backing, batting, and quilt top; baste. Quilt as desired. Quilt shown was quilted with ribbon designs, meandering in quilt center background, and with leaf designs in borders (*Quilting Diagram*).
3. Join 2¼"-wide blue print strips into 1 continuous piece for straight-grain French-fold binding. Add binding to quilt. ✳

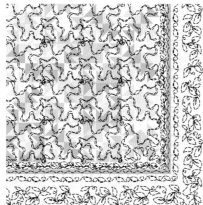

Quilting Diagram

DESIGNER

Amanda Murphy has worked as a graphic designer and an art director while continuing to sketch and sew her own designs. Amanda loves quilting because it marries her passion for design and her enthusiasm for handwork.

Color Play

Mix and match bright colors with classic geometric
black-and-white prints to create this quilt with a real wow factor.

PROJECT RATING: EASY
Size: 60" × 72"
Blocks: 20 (12") blocks

MATERIALS

4 fat quarters★ assorted prints in
medium and dark values of red,
green, and blue

20 fat eighths★★ assorted prints in
dark, medium, and light values of
red, yellow, green, teal, turquoise,
violet, pink, blue, and purple

⅞ yard black print #1 for blocks

1⅛ yards black print #2 for blocks
and outer border

⅝ yard black print #3 for blocks

½ yard black print #4 for blocks

1⅞ yards black solid for blocks and
inner border

4 yards backing fabric

Twin-size quilt batting

★fat quarter = 18" × 20"

★★fat eighth = 9" × 20"

Cutting

Measurements include ¼" seam
allowances. Border strips are exact
length needed. You may want to make
them longer to allow for piecing
variations. To make quilt shown, refer
to *Color Key and Cutting Chart* on
page 16 to cut assorted prints, or design
your own color scheme and use cutting
instructions.

From fat quarters, cut a total of:

• 4 sets of 5 matching (3⅞") squares.
Cut squares in half diagonally to make
4 sets of 10 matching half-square A
triangles.

• 4 sets of 10 matching (2") C squares.

• 2 sets of 4 matching (2") C squares.

From fat eighths, cut a total of:

• 24 sets of 10 matching (2") C squares.

• 6 sets of 4 matching (2") C squares.

From black print #1 print, cut:

• 2 (3⅞"-wide) strips. From strips, cut
20 (3⅞") squares. Cut squares in half
diagonally to make 40 half-square A
triangles.

• 8 (2"-wide) strips. From strips, cut 80
(2" × 3½") B rectangles.

From black print #2 print, cut:

• 6 (5"-wide) strips. Piece strips to make
2 (5" × 60½") side outer borders and
2 (5" × 48½") top and bottom outer
borders.

• 2 (2"-wide) strips. From strips, cut 40
(2") C squares.

From black print #3 print, cut:

• 8 (2"-wide) strips. From strips, cut 80
(2" × 3½") B rectangles.

From black print #4 print, cut:

• 2 (3½"-wide) strips. From strips, cut
20 (3½") D squares.

• 2 (2"-wide) strips. From strips, cut 40
(2") C squares.

From black solid, cut:

• 7 (2¼"-wide) strips for binding.

• 23 (2"-wide) strips. From 17 strips, cut
80 (2" × 3½") B rectangles and 192
(2") C squares. Piece remaining strips to
make 2 (2" × 60½") side inner borders
and 2 (2" × 48½") top and bottom
inner borders.

			A Triangles	C Squares
Fat Quarters		dark blue	10	14
		medium blue	10	10
		medium red	10	14
		medium green	10	10
Fat Eighths		dark red		10
		medium red		10
		light red		24
		dark yellow		24
		light yellow		14
		dark green		14
		medium green		14
		light green		10
		dark purple		10
		light purple		10
		dark violet		10
		medium violet		10
		light violet		20
		dark teal		10
		medium teal		10
		medium turquoise		10
		light turquoise		10
		light blue		24
		dark pink		10
		medium pink		10

Color Key and Cutting Chart

Block Assembly

1. Join 1 print A triangle and 1 black print #1 A triangle as shown in *Triangle-Square Diagrams*. Make 40 triangle-squares.

Triangle-Square Diagrams

2. Join 1 triangle square, 2 black print #1 B rectangles, and 1 print C square as shown in *Block Unit 1 Diagrams*. Make 4 sets of 10 matching Block Unit 1.

Block Unit 1 Diagrams

3. Join 1 black print #2 C square, 1 black print #4 C square, and 2 print C squares as shown in *Four Patch Unit 1 Diagrams*. Make 4 sets of 10 matching Four Patch Unit 1.

Four Patch Unit 1 Diagrams

4. Join 1 Four Patch Unit 1, 2 black print #3 B rectangles, and 1 black print #4 C square as shown in *Block Unit 2 Diagrams*. Make 4 sets of 10 matching Block Unit 2.

Block Unit 2 Diagrams

5. Join 2 black solid C squares and 2 print C squares as shown in *Four Patch Unit 2 Diagrams*. Make 8 sets of 10 matching Four Patch Unit 2.

Four Patch Unit 2 Diagrams

6. Join 1 Four Patch Unit 2 and 1 black solid B rectangle as shown in *Side Unit Diagrams*. Make 8 sets of 10 matching Side Units.
NOTE: Half of each set of Side Units are reversed as shown.

Side Unit Diagrams

7. Lay out 2 Block Unit 1, 2 Block Unit 2, 4 Side Units, and 1 black print #4 D square as shown in *Block Assembly Diagram*. Join into rows; join rows to complete 1 block *(Block Diagrams)*. Make 20 blocks in colors as shown.

Quilt Assembly

1. Lay out blocks as shown in *Quilt Top Assembly Diagram*.

2. Join blocks into rows; join rows to complete quilt center.

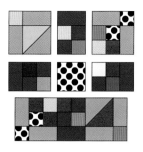

Block Assembly Diagram

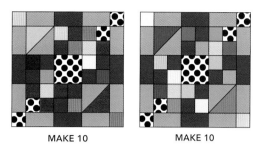

Block Diagrams

MAKE 10   MAKE 10

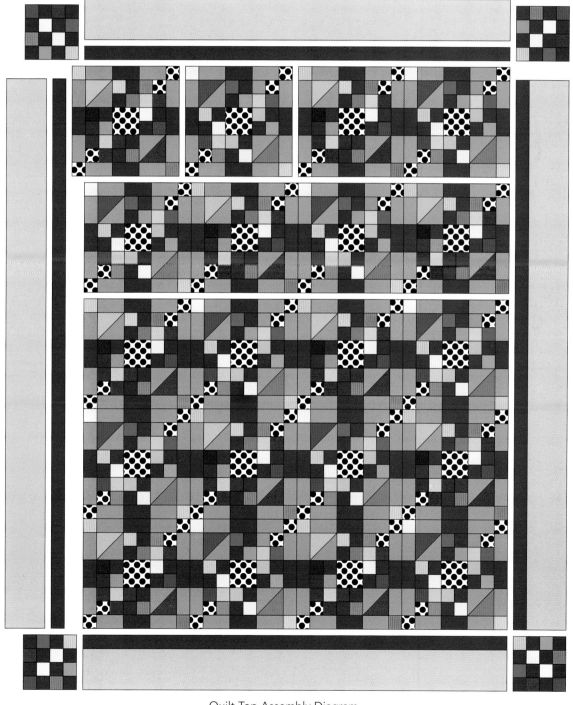

Quilt Top Assembly Diagram

3. Referring to *Quilt Top Assembly Diagram*, join 8 black solid C squares and 8 print C squares to make 1 Border Corner Unit *(Border Corner Unit Diagrams)*. Make 4 Border Corner Units.

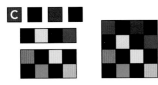

Border Corner Unit Diagrams

4. Join 1 black solid side inner border strip and 1 black print #2 outer border strip to make 1 pieced side border. Make 2 pieced side borders.

5. In the same manner, make pieced top and bottom borders.

6. Add pieced side borders to quilt center.

7. Add 1 Border Corner Unit to each end of pieced top and bottom borders. Add borders to quilt.

Finishing

1. Divide backing into 2 (2-yard) lengths. Join panels lengthwise. Seam will run horizontally.

2. Layer backing, batting, and quilt top; baste. Quilt as desired. Quilt shown was quilted with flowers in blocks, cable in inner border, and an allover design of curves and swirls in outer border *(Quilting Diagram)*.

3. Join 2¼"-wide black strips into 1 continuous piece for straight-grain French-fold binding. Add binding to quilt.

Quilting Diagram

DESIGNER

Author, teacher, fabric designer, and award-winning quiltmaker, Nancy Mahoney has enjoyed making quilts for more than twenty years. She enjoys combining traditional blocks and updated techniques to create dazzling quilts. Look for Nancy's twelfth book, *Kaleidoscope Paper Piecing*, in early 2012. Her latest title is *Fast, Fusible Flower Quilts*.

String Star

Marianne and Shon made this old favorite in 1930s prints. Use up narrow strips of leftover fabric to make the stars and accent them with your favorite color solid.

PROJECT RATING: INTERMEDIATE

Size: 66" × 72"

MATERIALS

2¾ yards blue solid for setting
    diamonds and borders
⅝ yard yellow print for binding
16 (¼-yard pieces) assorted prints for
    string stars
Fons & Porter's 60° Pyramids Ruler
    or template material
Fons & Porter's 60° Diamonds Ruler
    or template material
4 yards backing fabric
Twin-size quilt batting

Cutting

Measurements include ¼" seam allowances. Border strips are exact length needed. You may want to make them longer to allow for piecing variations. If you are not using Fons & Porter's 60° Pyramids and Fons & Porter's 60° Diamonds rulers, make templates from the patterns on pages 25 and 26.

From blue solid, cut:

• 5 (5¾"-wide) strips. From strips, cut 23 (5¾") diamonds. (See *Sew Easy: Cutting 60° Diamonds and Pyramids* on page 27 for instructions to cut diamonds.)
• 2 (5¾"-wide) strips. From strips, cut 4 (5¾" × 18⅞") rectangles. Trim both ends of rectangles at 60-degree angle as shown in *Trapezoid Cutting Diagrams*.

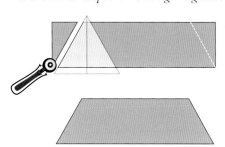

Trapezoid Cutting Diagrams

• 1 (5¾"-wide) strip. From strip, cut 2 (5¾" × 18½") rectangles. Referring to *Half Trapezoid Cutting Diagrams*, measure 11" from top left corner and cut strip at a 60-degree angle to make 2 half trapezoids. In a similar manner, measure 11" from bottom left corner and cut 2 reverse half trapezoids.

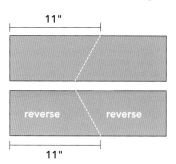

Half Trapezoid Cutting Diagrams

• 7 (5½"-wide) strips. Piece strips to make 2 (5½" × 66½") top and bottom outer borders and 2 (5½" × 62½") side outer borders.
• 3 (2½"-wide) strips. Piece strips to make 2 (2½" × 52½") top and bottom inner borders.

From yellow print, cut:
- 8 (2¼"-wide) strips for binding.

From each ¼-yard piece, cut:
- 5 strips ranging in width from 1¼"–2¼" for strip sets.

Cutting Triangles

1. Join strips randomly by color and width to make strip sets at least 6" wide *(Strip Set Diagram)*. Make 16 strip sets.

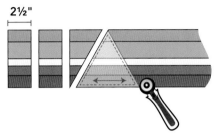

2½"

Strip Set Diagram

2. Referring to *Sew Easy: Cutting 60° Diamonds and Pyramids* on page 27, cut 112 triangles and 40 (2½"-wide) border segments from strip sets.

Quilt Center Assembly

1. Referring to *Quilt Top Assembly Diagram*, join 3 triangles, 2 trapezoids, 1 half trapezoid, and 1 reverse half trapezoid to complete Row 1. Make 2 Row 1.

2. Lay out 4 diamonds and 30 triangles as shown in Row 2. Join pieces into diagonal segments; join segments to complete Row 2. Make 2 Row 2.

3. In the same manner, make 2 Row 3 and 1 Row 4. Join rows to complete quilt center.

4. Trim top and bottom of quilt center ¼" from star points as shown.

Quilt Assembly

1. Join border segments end to end to make one long strip. From strip, cut 2 (2½" × 58½") pieced side inner borders and 2 (2½" × 56½") pieced top and bottom inner borders.

2. Add blue top and bottom inner borders to quilt center as shown in *Quilt Top Assembly Diagram*.

3. Add pieced side inner borders to quilt center. Add pieced top and bottom inner borders to quilt.

4. Repeat for blue outer borders.

Finishing

1. Divide backing into 2 (2-yard) lengths. Join panels lengthwise. Seams will run horizontally.

2. Layer backing, batting, and quilt top; baste. Quilt as desired. Quilt shown was quilted with feather designs in blue diamonds and borders and concentric triangles in pieced triangles *(Quilting Diagram)*.

3. Join 2¼"-wide yellow print strips into 1 continuous piece for straight-grain French-fold binding. Add binding to quilt.

Quilting Diagram

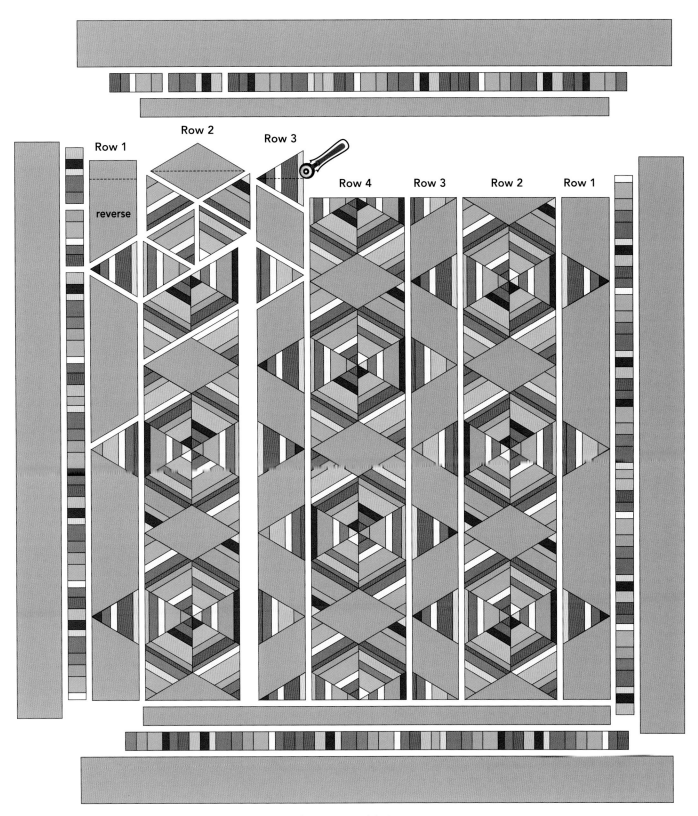

Row 2

Row 1

reverse

Row 3

Row 4   Row 3   Row 2   Row 1

Quilt Top Assembly Diagram

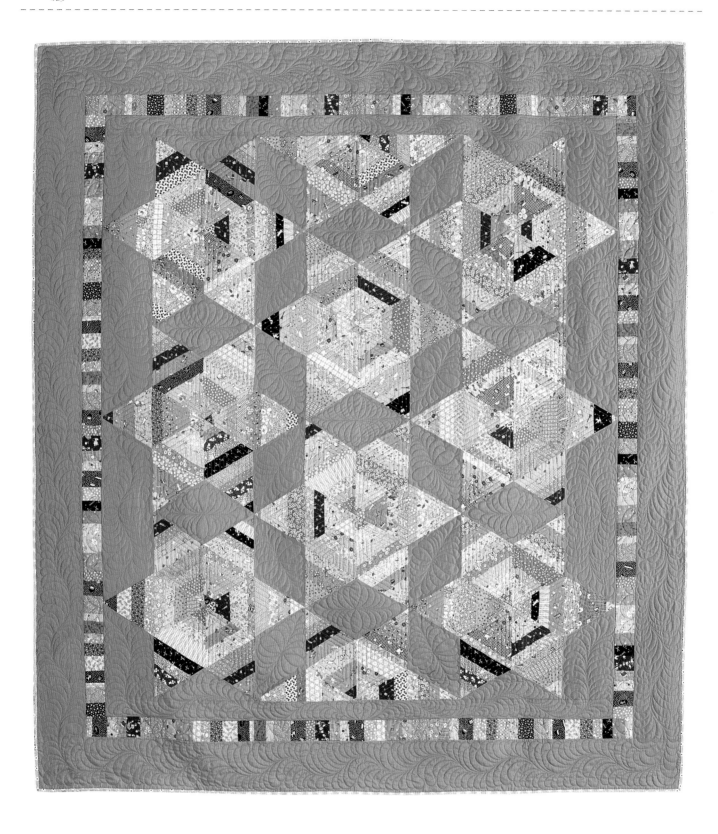

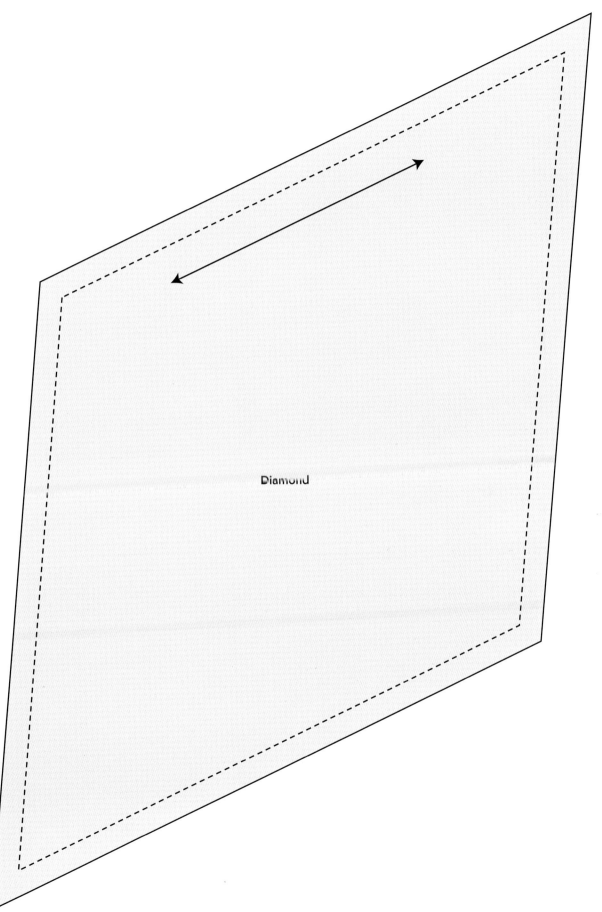

Diamond

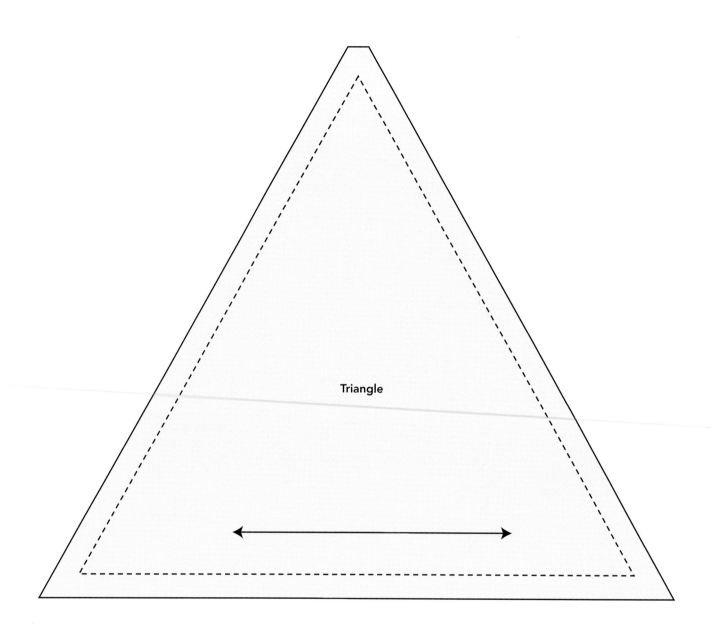

Triangle

Sew *Easy*™

Cutting 60° Diamonds and Pyramids

Use the Fons & Porter 60° Diamonds Ruler and 60° Pyramids Ruler to make easy work of cutting pieces.

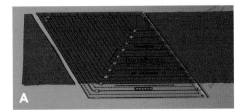 

  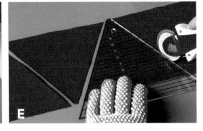

Diamonds

1. To cut diamonds, cut strip desired width (for *String Star,* cut strips 5¾" wide).

2. Referring to strip width numbers along lower section of Fons & Porter 60° Diamonds Ruler, find the line on the ruler that corresponds to the width of strip you cut.

3. Beginning at left end of fabric strip, place ruler so bottom line for desired size diamond is aligned with bottom edge of strip, and cut along left side of ruler (*Photo A*).

> ### Sew **Smart**™
> To cut the maximum number of pieces from a fabric strip, open out the strip so you will be cutting through a single layer. To cut many pieces, layer several strips and cut them at the same time. —Liz

4. Move ruler to the right; align desired line of ruler with slanted edge and bottom edge of strip. Cut along right slanted edge of ruler to cut diamond (*Photo B*).

5. Repeat Step #4 to cut required number of diamonds.

Pyramids

1. To cut pyramids (triangles), cut strip desired width (for *String Star,* cut strips 5¾" wide).

2. Referring to strip width numbers along lower section of Fons & Porter 60° Pyramids Ruler, find the line on the ruler that corresponds to the width of strip you cut.

3. Beginning at left end of fabric strip, place ruler atop strip so line on ruler is along bottom edge of fabric strip. Trim along left slanted edge of ruler (*Photo C*).

> ### Sew **Smart**™
> If you cut left-handed, work from the right end of the fabric strip and begin by cutting along the right edge of the ruler. —Marianne

4. Cut along right slanted edge of ruler to cut one pyramid triangle.

5. To cut second pyramid triangle, rotate ruler so solid line is on top edge of strip and angled side of ruler is aligned with slanted edge of strip. Cut along slanted edge of ruler (*Photo D*).

6. Continue in this manner to cut required number of Pyramids (*Photo E*).

Hello, Garden

This delightful quilt is made with precut 2½"-wide strips. Buy a package
or trade strips with your friends, choose a coordinating solid fabric for the background,
and start stitching—you'll be done in no time.

PROJECT RATING: EASY

Size. 40" × 54"

Blocks: 72 (6") blocks

MATERIALS

36 (2½"-wide) strips assorted prints
in green, pink, and turquoise (or
1 Jelly Roll™★)

1¾ yards white solid

3 yards backing fabric

Twin-size quilt batting

★Jelly Roll™ = 40 (2½" × 45")
strips

Cutting

Measurements include ¼" seam
allowances.

**From 2½"-wide print strips, cut a
total of:**

- 72 matching sets of 2 (2½") A squares
  and 1 (2½" × 6½") B
  rectangle.

From white solid, cut:

- 18 (2½"-wide) strips. From strips, cut
  288 (2½") A squares.
- 6 (2¼"-wide) strips for binding.

Block Assembly

1. Lay out 1 B rectangle, 2 matching
   print A squares, and 4 white A squares
   as shown in *Block Assembly Diagram*.

Block Assembly Diagram

2. Join into rows; join rows to complete
   1 block *(Block Diagram)*. Make 72
   blocks.

Block Diagram

Quilt Assembly

1. Lay out blocks as shown in *Quilt Top
   Assembly Diagram* on page 30.
2. Join blocks into rows; join rows to
   complete quilt top.

Finishing

1. Divide backing into 2 (1½-yard)
   lengths. Cut 1 piece in half lengthwise to make 2 narrow panels. Join 1
   narrow panel to wider panel. Seam
   will run horizontally. Remaining
   panel is extra and can be used to make
   a hanging sleeve.

Quilt Top Assembly Diagram

2. Layer backing, batting, and quilt top; baste. Quilt as desired. Quilt shown was quilted with an overall swirl design *(Quilting Diagram)*.

3. Join 2¼"-wide white strips into 1 continuous piece for straight-grain French-fold binding. Add binding to quilt.

Quilting Diagram

DESIGNER

Cherri House creates quilts using simple, traditional blocks with a modern twist. She has a pattern design business called Cherry House Quilts, and is the author of *City Quilts*, published by C&T Publishing. ✳

TRIED & TRUE

Is your style more traditional?
We used this collection of fabrics called Tied Up
(it features tie prints) by Dawn Spencer for Northcott.

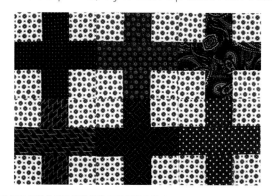

QUILT BY **Lynn Roddy Brown.**

Triple Four Patch

Lynn's alternate name for this quilt is Insanity 3044. It started with a bag of triple four patch blocks from a block exchange. Eight quilters each made ten sets of eight identical blocks and then traded them among the group. Lynn added a border and sashing to make her version unique.

PROJECT RATING: INTERMEDIATE

Size: 68¼" × 81¾"

Blocks: 120 (6") blocks

MATERIALS

7 fat quarters★ assorted dark prints

14 fat quarters★ assorted medium/ dark prints

7 fat quarters★ assorted light prints

1¾ yards blue print for border blocks

½ yard gold print for border blocks

¾ yard brown print for binding

¾ yard dark green print for border sashing

1 fat quarter★ medium green print for cornerstones

1¼ yards multicolor print for center sashing

5 yards backing fabric

Twin-size quilt batting

★fat quarter = 18" × 20"

Cutting

Measurements include ¼" seam allowances.

From dark print fat quarters, cut a total of:

• 80 (1¼"-wide) strips for strip sets.

From medium/dark print fat quarters, cut a total of:

• 40 (3½"-wide) strips. From strips, cut 80 sets of 2 matching (3½") C squares.

• 40 (2"-wide) strips. From strips, cut 80 sets of 4 matching (2") B squares.

From light print fat quarters, cut a total of:

• 80 (1¼"-wide) strips for strip sets.

From remainders of light print fat quarters, cut a total of:

• 4 (1¼"-wide) strips. From strips, cut 49 (1¼") A squares.

From blue print, cut:

• 8 (3½"-wide) strips. From strips, cut 80 (3½") C squares.

• 8 (2"-wide) strips. From strips, cut 160 (2") B squares.

• 10 (1¼"-wide) strips for strip sets.

From gold print, cut:

• 11 (1¼"-wide) strips. From 1 strip, cut 22 (1¼") A squares. Remaining strips are for strip sets.

From brown print, cut:

• 9 (2¼"-wide) strips for binding.

From dark green print, cut:

• 3 (6½"-wide) strips. From strips, cut 84 (6½" × 1¼") D rectangles.

From medium green print fat quarter, cut:

• 6 (1¼"-wide) strips. From strips, cut 72 (1¼") A squares.

From multicolor print, cut:

• 6 (6½"-wide) strips. From strips, cut 178 (6½" × 1¼") D rectangles.

Block Assembly

1. Join 1 light print strip and 1 dark print strip as shown in *Strip Set Diagram*. Make 80 strip sets. From each strip set, cut 8 (1¼"-wide) segments.

1¼"

Strip Set Diagram

2. Referring to *Four Patch Unit Diagrams*, join 2 matching segments to make 1 Four Patch Unit. Make 4 matching Four Patch Units.

Four Patch Unit Diagrams

3. Join 2 Four Patch Units and 2 matching B squares as shown in *Double Four Patch Unit Diagrams*. Make 2 Double Four Patch Units.

Double Four Patch Unit Diagrams

4. Lay out Double Four Patch Units and 2 matching C squares as shown in *Block Assembly Diagrams*. Join to complete 1 block *(Block Diagram)*. Make 80 blocks.

Block Assembly Diagrams

Block Diagram

Border Block Assembly

1. Join 1 gold print strip and 1 blue print strip as shown in *Strip Set Diagram*. Make 10 strip sets. From strip sets, cut 320 (1¼"-wide) segments.

1¼"

Strip Set Diagram

2. Referring to *Four Patch Unit Diagrams*, join 2 segments to make 1 Four Patch Unit. Make 160 Four Patch Units.

Four Patch Unit Diagrams

3. Join 2 Four Patch Units and 2 blue print B squares as shown in *Double Four Patch Unit Diagrams*. Make 80 Double Four Patch Units.

Double Four Patch Unit Diagrams

4. Lay out 2 Double Four Patch Units and 2 blue print C squares as shown in *Border Block Assembly Diagrams*. Join to complete 1 block *(Border Block Diagram)*. Make 40 border blocks.

Block Assembly Diagrams

Block Diagram

Quilt Assembly

1. Lay out blocks, D rectangles, and A squares as shown in *Quilt Top Assembly Diagram*.

2. Join into rows; join rows to complete quilt top.

> ### Sew **Smart**™
> **Using sashing and cornerstones helps keep the quilt square.**
> —Lynn

Finishing

1. Divide backing into 2 (2½-yard) lengths. Cut 1 piece in half lengthwise to make 2 narrow panels. Join 1 narrow panel to each side of wider panel; press seam allowances toward narrow panels.

2. Layer backing, batting, and quilt top; baste. Quilt as desired. Quilt shown was quilted in the ditch around blocks and with allover meandering in blocks *(Quilting Diagram)*.

3. Join 2¼"-wide brown print strips into 1 continuous piece for straight-grain French-fold binding. Add binding to quilt.

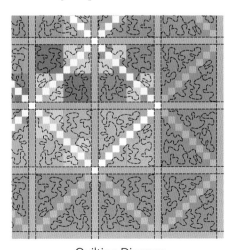

Quilting Diagram

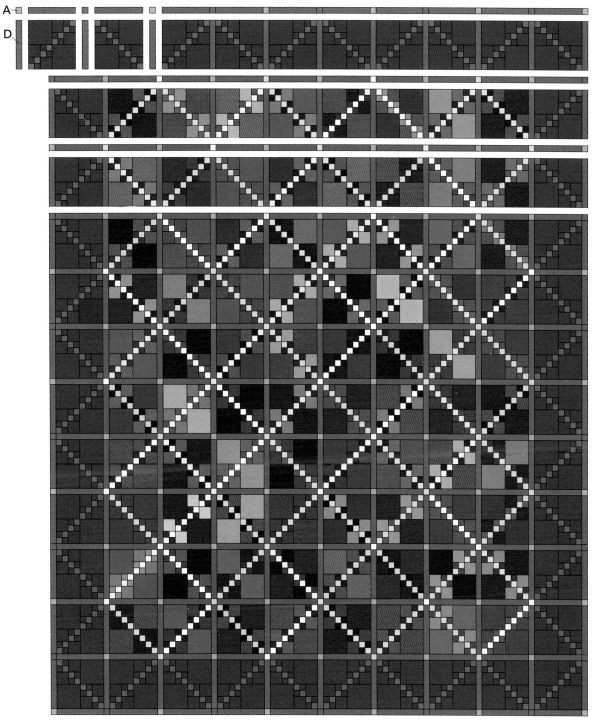

A

D

Quilt Top Assembly Diagram

DESIGNER

Lynn Roddy Brown is a master at making scrap quilts, which she loves
because they give her the opportunity to use many different fabrics. Lynn is
a member of a quilting bee that trades blocks for making scrap quilts, and is
the author of three books, all published by Martingale & Co.

Petals

Natalia Bonner has created a time-worn, slightly faded look with a simple idea and a great collection of fabrics. The petal pieces are big and fun to machine appliqué.

PROJECT RATING: INTERMEDIATE

Size: 79½" × 79½"

Blocks: 25 (13½") blocks

MATERIALS

5¼ yards white solid for block backgrounds

2 yards white print for sashing and border

7 fat quarters★ assorted red prints for blocks

5 fat quarters★ assorted yellow prints for blocks

9 fat quarters★ assorted blue prints for blocks

3 fat eighths★★ assorted white prints for blocks

4 fat quarters★ assorted light red and blue prints for blocks

¾ yard red print for binding

Paper-backed fusible web

7½ yards backing fabric

Full-size quilt batting

★fat quarter = 18" × 20"

★★fat eighth = 9" × 20"

Cutting

Measurements include ¼" seam allowances. Border strips are exact length needed. You may want to make them longer to allow for piecing variations. Patterns for Petal and Circles are on pages 39–40. Follow manufacturer's instructions for using fusible web.

From white solid, cut:

• 13 (14"-wide) strips. From strips, cut 25 (14") A squares.

From white print, cut:

• 26 (2½"-wide) strips. From 10 strips, cut 20 (2½" × 14") vertical sashing strips. Piece remaining strips to make 2 (2½" × 80") top and bottom borders, 2 (2½" × 76") side borders, and 4 (2½" × 76") horizontal sashing strips.

From red print fat quarters, cut a total of:

• 80 Petals.

From blue print fat quarters, cut a total of:

• 110 Petals.

From yellow print fat quarters, cut a total of:

• 50 Petals.

From white print fat eighths, cut a total of:

• 10 Petals.

From remainders of red, blue, yellow, and white prints, cut a total of:

• 25 Large Circles.

• 25 Small Circles.

From light blue and light red print fat quarters, cut a total of:

• 100 (3") B squares.

From red print, cut:

• 9 (2¼"-wide) strips for binding.

Block Assembly

1. Referring to *Block Assembly Diagrams*, place 1 light red or blue print B square atop 1 white A square, right sides facing. Stitch diagonally from corner to corner as shown. Trim ¼" beyond stitching. Press open to reveal triangle. Repeat for remaining corners to complete 1 block background.

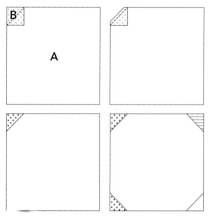

Block Assembly Diagrams

2. Position 10 red Petals, 1 large Circle, and 1 small Circle atop block background; fuse in place. Machine appliqué flower on block background, using matching thread and blanket stitch, to complete 1 block *(Block Diagram)*. Make 8 red blocks, 11 blue blocks, 5 yellow blocks, and 1 white block.

Block Diagram

Quilt Assembly

1. Lay out blocks and sashing strips as shown in *Quilt Top Assembly Diagram*. Join into rows; join rows to complete quilt center.

2. Add white print side borders to quilt center. Add white print top and bottom borders to quilt.

Finishing

1. Divide backing into 3 (2½-yard) lengths. Cut 1 piece in half lengthwise to make 2 narrow panels. Join 1 narrow panel to wider panels. Remaining panel is extra and can be used to make a hanging sleeve.

2. Layer backing, batting, and quilt top; baste. Quilt as desired. Quilt shown was quilted with swirl designs in sashing and borders, and small circles in block background *(Quilting Diagram)*.

3. Join 2¼"-wide red print strips into 1 continuous piece for straight-grain French-fold binding. Add binding to quilt.

Quilting Diagram

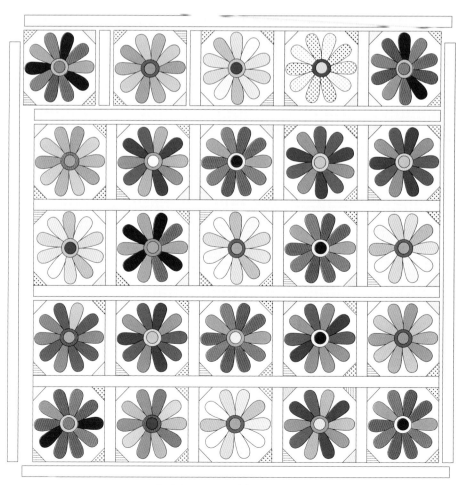

Quilt Top Assembly Diagram

DESIGNER

Natalia Bonner grew up watching ladies sew at her mother's custom curtain shop. She kept scraps and started making her own quilts, one of which won a ribbon at a state fair. She is now a prize-winning quilter and teacher of machine quilting and her raw-edge appliqué technique.

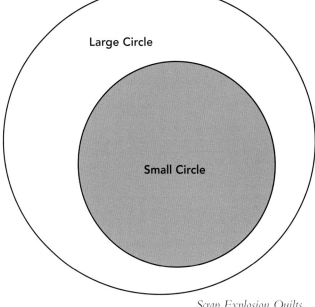

Large Circle

Small Circle

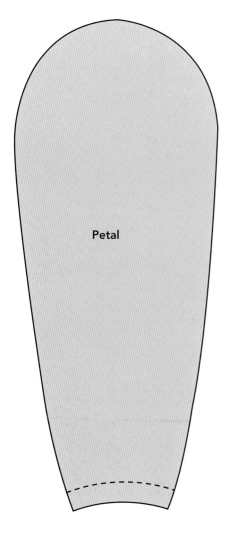

Petal

SIZE OPTIONS

	Crib (48½" × 48½")	Queen (95" × 95")
Blocks	9	36
Setting	3 × 3	6 × 6

Materials

	Crib	Queen
White Solid	2 yards	7 yards
White Print	1 yard	2½ yards
Red Prints	3 fat quarters★	10 fat quarters★
Yellow Prints	3 fat quarters★	8 fat quarters★
Blue Prints	3 fat quarters★	14 fat quarters★
White Prints	---	3 fat eighths★★
Light Prints	3 fat eighths★	7 fat quarters★★
Binding Fabric	½ yard	⅞ yard
Backing Fabric	3 yards	9 yards
Batting	Twin-Size	King-Size

★fat quarter = 18" × 20"

★★fat eighth = 9" × 20"

Crib Size

Crib-Size Cutting

From white solid, cut:
- 5 (14"-wide) strips. From strips, cut 9 (14") A squares.

From white print, cut:
- 10 (3"-wide) strips. From 3 strips, cut 6 (2½" × 14") vertical sashing strips. Piece remaining strips to make 2 (2½" × 49") top and bottom borders, 2 (2½" × 45") side borders, and 4 (2½" × 45") horizontal sashing strips.

From red print fat quarters, cut a total of:
- 30 Petals.

From blue print fat quarters, cut a total of:
- 30 Petals.

From yellow print fat quarters, cut a total of:
- 30 Petals.

From light print fat eighths, cut a total of:
- 36 (3") B squares.

From remainders of red, blue, yellow, and white prints, cut a total of:
- 9 Large Circles.
- 9 Small Circles.

From binding fabric, cut:
- 6 (2¼"-wide) strips for binding.

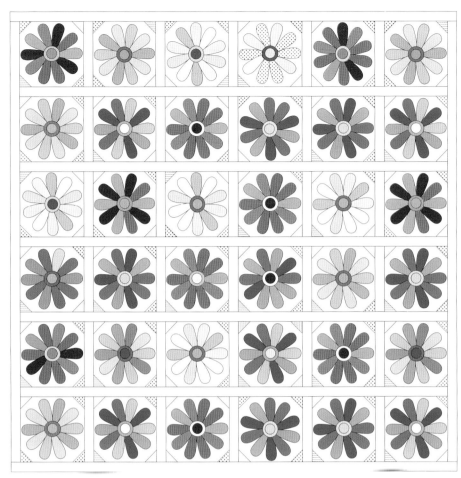

Queen Size

Queen-Size Cutting

From white solid, cut:

• 18 (14"-wide) strips. From strips, cut 36 (14") A squares.

From white print, cut:

• 29 (3"-wide) strips. From 15 strips, cut 30 (2½" × 14") vertical sashing strips. Piece remaining strips to make 2 (2½" × 95½") top and bottom borders, 2 (2½" × 91½") side borders, and 4 (2½" × 91½") horizontal sashing strips.

From red print fat quarters, cut a total of:

• 100 Petals.

From blue print fat quarters, cut a total of:

• 200 Petals.

From yellow print fat quarters, cut a total of:

• 50 Petals.

From white print fat eighths, cut a total of:

• 10 Petals.

From remainders of red, blue, yellow, and white prints, cut a total of:

• 36 Large Circles.

• 36 Small Circles.

From light print fat quarters, cut a total of:

• 144 (3") B squares.

From binding fabric, cut:

• 11 (2¼"-wide) strips for binding.

Feedsack Flowers

Stitch these hexagons log cabin style, and then join them into rows. It's much easier than it looks!

PROJECT RATING: INTERMEDIATE

Size: 73" × 91"

Blocks: 60 (9") Hexagon blocks

MATERIALS

⅝ yard each of 14 assorted prints for blocks and border

¾ yard yellow solid for block centers

2 yards cream solid

⅞ yard yellow print for blocks and inner border

1 yard green print for blocks, outer border, and binding

Fons & Porter Hexagon Ruler (optional) or template material

Fons & Porter 60° Pyramid Ruler (optional) or template material

5½ yards backing fabric

Full-size quilt batting

Cutting

Measurements include ¼" seam allowances. Border strips are exact length needed. You may want to make them longer to allow for piecing variations. Instructions are written for using the Fons & Porter Hexagon Ruler and 60° Pyramid Ruler. For instructions on using these rulers, go to FonsandPorter.com/60HexPyramid. If not using these rulers, make hexagon and triangle templates from patterns on page 45.

From each print, cut:

• 7 (1¾"-wide) strips. From strips, cut 4 (1¾" × 7¼") D rectangles, 20 (1¾" × 5¾") C rectangles, 20 (1¾" × 4¼") B rectangles, and 4 (1¾" × 2¾") A rectangles.

• 3 (1½"-wide) strips. From strips, cut 21 (1½" × 5½") E rectangles.

From yellow solid, cut:

• 6 (3½"-wide) strips. From strips, cut 60 hexagons.

From cream solid, cut:

• 10 (4½"-wide) strips. From strips, cut 118 (60°) triangles.

• 7 (2½"-wide) strips. Piece strips to make 2 (2½" × 74½") side inner borders and 2 (2½" × 60½") top and bottom inner borders.

From yellow print, cut:

• 8 (2"-wide) strips. Piece strips to make 2 (2" × 78½") side middle borders and 2 (2" × 63½") top and bottom middle borders.

• 4 (1¾"-wide) strips. From strips, cut 2 (1¾" × 7¼") D rectangles, 10 (1¾" × 5¾") C rectangles, 10 (1¾" × 4¼") B rectangles, and 2 (1¾" × 2¾") A rectangles.

• 1 (1½"-wide) strip. From strip, cut 7 (1½" × 5½") E rectangles.

From green print, cut:

• 9 (2¼"-wide) strips for binding.

• 4 (1¾"-wide) strips. From strips, cut 2 (1¾" × 7¼") D rectangles, 10 (1¾" × 5¾") C rectangles, 10 (1¾" × 4¼") B rectangles, and 2 (1¾" × 2¾") A rectangles.

• 1 (1½"-wide) strip. From strip, cut 7 (1½" × 5½") E rectangles.

Block Assembly

1. Make 60 Hexagon blocks as shown in *Sew Easy: Log Cabin Hexagons* on page 47.

2. Add 2 cream solid triangles to each of 52 Hexagon blocks as shown in *Hexagon Unit Diagrams*. Remaining blocks are for top and bottom rows.

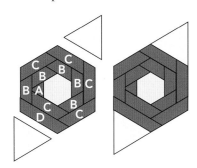

Hexagon Unit Diagrams

Pieced Border Assembly

1. Join 81 assorted E rectangles to make 1 side outer border as shown in *Quilt Top Assembly Diagram*. Make 2 side outer borders.

2. In the same manner, join 73 assorted E rectangles to make top outer border. Repeat for bottom outer border.

Quilt Assembly

1. Lay out Hexagon Units, remaining blocks, and remaining cream solid triangles as shown in *Quilt Top Assembly Diagram*.

2. Join into vertical rows; join rows. Trim top and bottom edges, ¼" beyond points of hexagons as shown to complete quilt center.

3. Add cream solid side inner borders to quilt center. Add top and bottom inner borders to quilt.

4. Repeat for yellow print middle borders and pieced outer borders.

Quilt Top Assembly Diagram

Finishing

1. Divide backing into 2 (2¾-yard) lengths. Cut 1 piece in half lengthwise to make 2 narrow panels. Join 1 narrow panel to each side of wider panel; press seam allowances toward narrow panels.

2. Layer backing, batting, and quilt top; baste. Quilt as desired. Quilt shown was quilted with an allover loopy design *(Quilting Diagram)*.

3. Join 2¼"-wide green print strips into 1 continuous piece for straight-grain French-fold binding. Add binding to quilt.

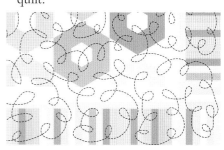

Quilting Diagram

TRIED & TRUE

We changed the Hexagon Log Cabin block just a little by using three prints for each block. Fabrics are from the A La Maison collection by Terri Conrad Designs for Robert Kaufman.

DESIGNER

Betsy DeFazio enjoys selecting colors and fabrics for her new designs. When she's not quilting, she's reading or golfing, and she says, "My seven grandkids keep me in stitches, one way or another!"

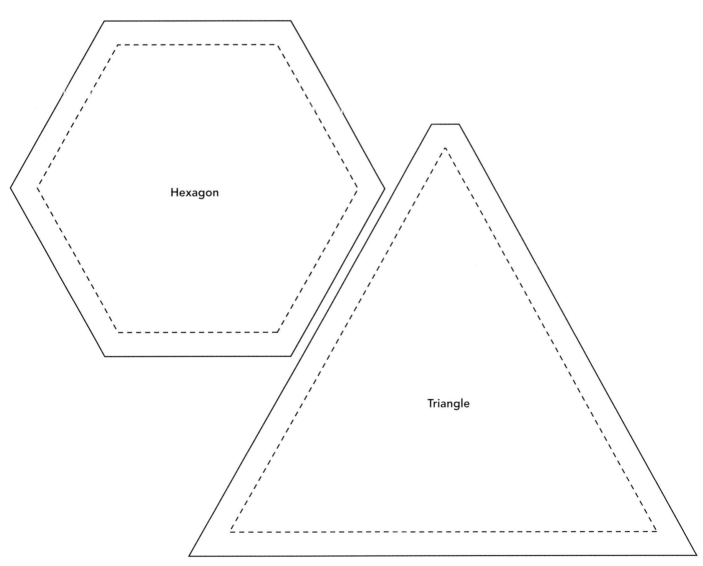

Hexagon

Triangle

Log Cabin Hexagons

Make log-cabin style hexagon blocks using this easy method.

1. Center 1 print A rectangle atop one edge of center hexagon (*Photo A*). Stitch rectangle to hexagon; press seam allowance toward rectangle.
2. Trim ends of rectangle even with edge of hexagon (*Photo B*).
3. Working clockwise, stitch 1 print B rectangle to hexagon. Trim end of rectangle, aligning edge of ruler with edge of hexagon as shown in *Photo C*. Trim opposite end of rectangle in the same manner.
4. Continue adding rectangles to hexagon, trimming ends of rectangles after each is added, to complete block (*Photo D*).

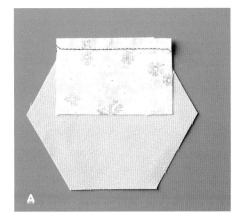

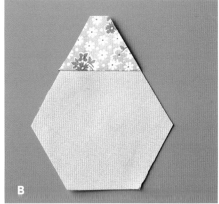

Friendship Rings

Careful placement of the highly contrasting navy and beige print pieces in two different blocks creates the illusion of overlapping rings. The rest of the quilt is scrappy.

PROJECT RATING: INTERMEDIATE

Size: 69" × 78"

Blocks: 56 (9") blocks

MATERIALS

2⅞ yards navy print for blocks, border, and binding

2¼ yards beige print for blocks

16 fat quarters★ assorted prints in red, blue, green, yellow, purple, and teal for blocks

Template material

4¾ yards backing fabric

Twin-size quilt batting

Cutting

Measurements include ¼" seam allowances. Border strips are exact length needed. You may want to make them longer to allow for piecing variations. Patterns for D and E are on page 53.

From navy print, cut:

• 6 (3⅞"-wide) strips. From strips, cut 56 (3⅞") squares. Cut squares in half diagonally to make 112 half-square A triangles.

• 16 (3½"-wide) strips. From 8 strips, cut 112 D and 112 D reversed. Piece remaining strips to make 2 (3½" × 72½") side borders and 2 (3½" × 69½") top and bottom borders.

• 8 (2¼"-wide) strips for binding.

From beige print, cut:

• 4 (4¼"-wide) strips. From strips, cut 28 (4¼") squares. Cut squares in half diagonally in both directions to make 112 quarter-square B triangles.

• 6 (3⅞"-wide) strips. From strips, cut 56 (3⅞") squares. Cut squares in half diagonally to make 112 half-square A triangles.

• 10 (3½"-wide) strips. From strips, cut 112 E.

From assorted prints, cut a total of:

• 56 (2"-wide) strips for strip sets.

• 28 (4¼") squares. Cut squares in half diagonally in both directions to make 112 quarter-square B triangles.

• 28 matching pairs of (3⅞") squares. Cut squares in half diagonally to make 112 half-square A triangles.

• 56 (3½") C squares.

Block 1 Assembly

1. Join 1 navy print A triangle and 1 beige print A triangle as shown in *Triangle-Square Diagrams*. Make 112 triangle-squares.

Triangle-Square Diagrams

2. Join 1 print A triangle, 1 beige print B triangle, and 1 print B triangle as shown in *Side Unit Diagrams*. Make 28 sets of 4 matching Side Units.

Side Unit Diagrams

3. Lay out 4 triangle-squares, 1 set of Side Units, and 1 print C square as shown in *Block 1 Assembly Diagram*. Join into rows; join rows to complete 1 Block 1 *(Block 1 Diagram)*. Make 28 Block 1.

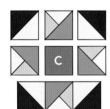

Block 1 Assembly Diagram

Block 1 Diagram

Block 2 Assembly

1. Join 2 print strips as shown in *Strip Set Diagram*. Make 28 strip sets. From strip sets, cut 224 (2"-wide) segments.

Strip Set Diagram

2. Join 2 segments as shown in *Four Patch Unit Diagrams*. Make 112 Four Patch Units.

Four Patch Unit Diagrams

3. Join 1 beige print E triangle, 1 navy print D triangle, and 1 navy print D triangle reversed as shown in *Star Point Unit Diagrams*. Make 112 Star Point Units.

Star Point Unit Diagrams

4. Lay out 4 Four Patch Units, 4 Star Point Units, and 1 print C square as shown in *Block 2 Assembly Diagram*. Join into rows; join rows to complete 1 Block 2 *(Block 2 Diagram)*. Make 28 Block 2.

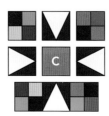

Block 2 Assembly Diagram

Block 2 Diagram

Quilt Assembly

1. Lay out blocks as shown in *Quilt Top Assembly Diagram* on page 51.

2. Join blocks into rows; join rows to complete quilt center.

3. Add navy print side borders to quilt center. Add navy print top and bottom borders to quilt.

Finishing

1. Divide backing into 2 (2⅜-yard) lengths. Cut 1 piece in half lengthwise to make 2 narrow panels. Join 1 narrow panel to each side of wider panel; press seam allowances toward narrow panels.

2. Layer backing, batting, and quilt top; baste. Quilt as desired. Quilt shown was quilted with an allover design of swirls in the center and feathers in the border *(Quilting Diagram)*.

3. Join 2¼"-wide navy print strips into 1 continuous piece for straight-grain French-fold binding. Add binding to quilt.

Quilting Diagram

Quilt Top Assembly Diagram

DESIGNER

Nancy McNally has been quilting for more than fifteen years. In addition to creating and publishing her own patterns, she teaches quilting and is a longarm quilter.

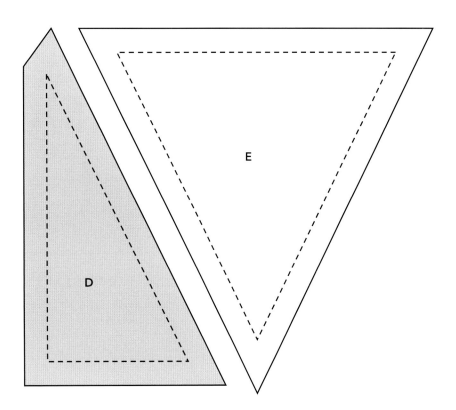

Around and Around

Bev Getschel used 1930s reproduction prints for her spinning Pinwheel blocks.
A touch of appliqué and scrappy borders complete this fun throw.

PROJECT RATING: INTERMEDIATE

Size: 60" × 72½"

Blocks: 10 (10") Pinwheel blocks

MATERIALS

3 yards cream solid

⅜ yard blue print for quilt center border

¾ yard red print for blocks, Flowers, and binding

½ yard green print for blocks and Leaves

½ yard each of 6 assorted prints in blue, red, green, and yellow

Paper-backed fusible web

4 yards backing fabric

Twin-size quilt batting

Cutting

Measurements include ¼" seam allowances. Patterns for Flower and Leaf are on page 58. Follow manufacturer's instructions for using fusible web. For step-by-step photos and a video, see *Sew Easy: Fusible Web Appliqué* on page 59 and at fonsandporter.com/fusiblewebapp.

From cream solid, cut:

• 2 (13⅞"-wide) strips. From strips, cut 4 (13⅞") squares. Cut squares in half diagonally to make 8 half-square D triangles.

• 1 (8⅜"-wide) strip. From strip, cut 4 (8⅜") squares. Cut squares in half diagonally in both directions to make 16 quarter-square H triangles. **NOTE:** Be sure to label these triangles H.

• 5 (5⅞"-wide) strips. From strips, cut 30 (5⅞") squares. Cut squares in half diagonally to make 60 half-square A triangles.

• 5 (3⅜"-wide) strips. From strips, cut 45 (3⅜") squares. Cut squares in half diagonally to make 90 half-square E triangles.

• 2 (3"-wide) strips. Piece strips to make 1 (3" × 50½") G rectangle.

• 5 (2½"-wide) strips. Piece strips to make 2 (2½" × 50½") top and bottom inner borders and 2 (2½" × 46½") side inner borders.

From blue print, cut:

• 4 (2½"-wide) strips. From strips, cut 2 (2½" × 33") C rectangles and 2 (2½" × 29") B rectangles.

From red print, cut:

• 1 (5⅞"-wide) strip. From strip, cut 2 (5⅞") squares. Cut squares in half diagonally to make 4 half-square A triangles.

• 7 (2¼"-wide) strips for binding.

• 4 Flowers.

From green print, cut:

- 1 (5⅞"-wide) strip. From strip, cut 2 (5⅞") squares. Cut squares in half diagonally to make 4 half-square A triangles.
- 24 Leaves.

From assorted prints and remainders of red and green prints, cut a total of:

- 4 Flowers.
- 8 Flower Centers.
- 45 (3⅜") squares. Cut squares in half diagonally to make 90 half-square E triangles.
- 13 matching pairs of (5⅞") squares. Cut squares in half diagonally to make 52 half-square A triangles.
- 4 (3") F squares.
- 8 (3") strips. Cut strips in half to make 16 (3" × 20") strips for outer border.

Block Assembly

1. Join 1 cream A triangle and 1 print A triangle as shown in *Triangle-Square Diagrams.* Make 60 large triangle-squares.

Triangle-Square Diagrams

2. Lay out 4 matching large triangle-squares as shown in *Pinwheel Block Assembly Diagram.* Join into rows; join rows to complete 1 Pinwheel block *(Pinwheel Block Diagram).* Make 10 Pinwheel blocks.

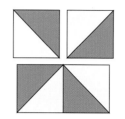

Pinwheel Block Assembly Diagram

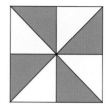

Pinwheel Block Diagram

Quilt Center Assembly

1. Lay out red Pinwheel block, 20 large triangle-squares, and 16 cream H triangles as shown in *Center Unit Diagrams.* Join into diagonal rows; join rows to make pieced center.

2. Add blue print B rectangles to pieced center. Add blue print C rectangles to complete Center Unit.

3. Join 1 Pinwheel block and 1 cream D triangle as shown in *Corner Unit Diagrams.* Trim triangle even with edge of block.

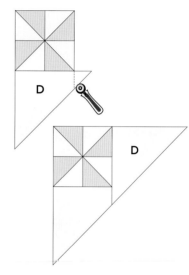

Corner Unit Diagrams

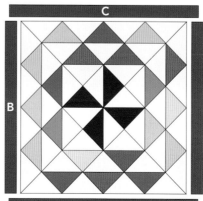

Center Unit Diagrams

4. Add 1 cream D triangle to complete 1 Corner Unit. Make 4 Corner Units.

5. Referring to *Quilt Center Diagram*, add Corner Units to Center Unit.

6. Arrange appliqué pieces atop quilt center; fuse in place. Machine appliqué pieces using black thread and blanket stitch.

Pieced Border Assembly

1. Join 1 cream E triangle and 1 print E triangle as shown in *Triangle-Square Diagrams* on page 56. Make 90 small triangle-squares.

2. Referring to *Quilt Top Assembly Diagram*, join 25 small triangle-squares as shown to make pieced side middle border. Make 2 pieced side middle borders.

3. Join 20 small triangle-squares and 2 print F squares as shown to make pieced top middle border. Repeat for pieced bottom middle border

4. Join 5 Pinwheel blocks, cream G rectangle, and cream top inner border to make pieced top inner border.

Quilt Assembly

1. Add cream side inner borders to quilt center.

2. Add pieced top inner border to quilt center. Add cream bottom inner border to quilt.

3. Add pieced side middle borders to quilt center. Add pieced top and bottom middle borders to quilt.

4. Join assorted (3"-wide) strips end to end to make 1 long strip. From strip, cut 2 (3" × 68") side outer borders and 2 (3" × 60½") top and bottom outer borders.

5. Add side outer borders to quilt center. Add top and bottom outer borders to quilt.

Quilt Center Diagram

Quilt Top Assembly Diagram

Finishing

1. Divide backing into 2 (2-yard) lengths. Join panels lengthwise. Seam will run horizontally.

2. Layer backing, batting, and quilt top; baste. Quilt as desired. Quilt shown was quilted with continuous curves in triangle-squares and feather and leaf designs in background areas (*Quilting Diagram*).

3. Join 2¼"-wide red print strips into 1 continuous piece for straight-grain French-fold binding. Add binding to quilt.

Quilting Diagram

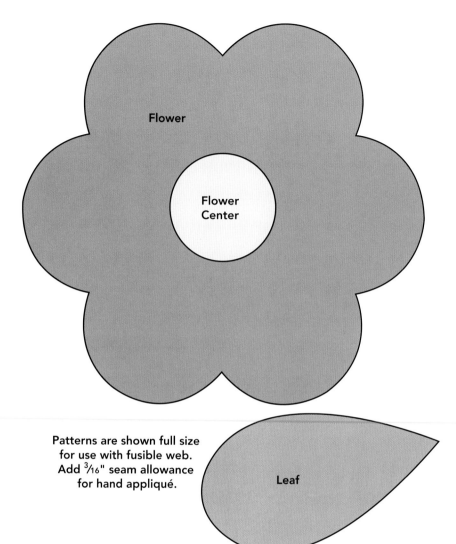

Flower

Flower Center

Patterns are shown full size for use with fusible web. Add ³⁄₁₆" seam allowance for hand appliqué.

Leaf

DESIGNER

Bev Getschel fell in love with quilting in 2003, after having sewn all her life. She is the winner of several awards, and is regularly published in quilting magazines.

TRIED & TRUE

The center medallion looks great in every style. Ours is made with trend-setting fabrics from Timeless Treasures. The fabric collection is Washi by Rashida Coleman-Hale.

Fusible Web Appliqué

For large shapes with fairly smooth edges, this appliqué technique works well. Fusing pieces to the background eliminates the need for basting.

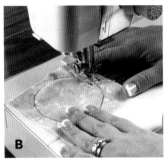

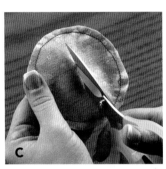

1. Trace appliqué shape onto fusible interfacing; cut out about ½" outside of drawn line *(Photo A)*.
2. Position interfacing atop appliqué with fusible side of interfacing against right side of fabric. Stitch on drawn line through both layers *(Photo B)*.
3. Trim away excess fabric, leaving a ¼" seam allowance. Cut a slit in interfacing to turn appliqué piece *(Photo C)*.
4. Turn piece right side out, place on non-stick appliqué pressing sheet, and press shape flat *(Photo D)*.
5. Lay out pieces on background fabric and fuse in place *(Photo E)*.
6. Appliqué pieces to background using either a hand or machine stitch.

> ## Sew **Smart**™
> For curved pieces, clip curves OR trim seam allowance with pinking shears to make the piece lie flat when it is turned right side out. —Liz

QUILT DESIGNED AND MADE BY **Liz Porter.**

HAND QUILTED BY THE **Ada Troyer Family.**

Barbed Wire

Liz says, "I used lots of my small scraps to make this zigzag quilt. The black print background perfectly highlights the many colors in the triangles."

PROJECT RATING: INTERMEDIATE

Size: 56½" × 85"

Blocks: 155 (4") Four Patch Units

MATERIALS

9 fat quarters★★ or 18 fat eighths★ assorted light prints

9 fat quarters★★ or 18 fat eighths★ assorted dark prints

2¾ yards black print for background

⅝ yard red print for binding

Fons & Porter Half & Quarter Ruler (optional)

5¼ yards backing fabric

Twin-size quilt batting

★fat eighth = 9" × 20"

★★fat quarter = 18" × 20"

Cutting

Measurements include ¼" seam allowances. Instructions are written for using the Fons & Porter Half & Quarter Ruler. If not using this ruler, follow cutting NOTES.

From assorted light prints, cut a total of:

• 52 (2½"-wide) strips. From strips, cut 620 half-square triangles

  NOTE: If not using the Fons & Porter Half & Quarter Ruler, cut 52 (2⅞"-wide) strips. From strips, cut 310 (2⅞") squares. Cut squares in half diagonally to make 620 half-square triangles.

From assorted dark prints, cut a total of:

• 52 (2½"-wide) strips. From strips, cut 620 half-square triangles.

  NOTE: If not using the Fons & Porter Half & Quarter Ruler, cut 52 (2⅞"-wide) strips. From strips, cut 310 (2⅞") squares. Cut squares in half diagonally to make 620 half-square triangles.

From black print, cut:

• 21 (4½"-wide) strips. From strips, cut 40 (4½" × 12½") A rectangles, 8 (4½" × 8½") B rectangles, and 42 (4½") C squares.

From red print, cut:

• 8 (2¼"-wide) strips for binding.

Zigzag Unit Assembly

1. Join 1 light print triangle and 1 dark print triangle as shown in *Triangle-Square Diagrams*. Make 620 triangle-squares.

Triangle-Square Diagrams

2. Join 4 triangle-squares as shown in *Four Patch Unit Diagrams*. Make 155 Four Patch Units.

Four Patch Unit Diagrams

3. Join 4 Four Patch Units, 1 black print A rectangle, and 1 black print C square as shown in *Unit 1 Diagrams*. Make 30 Unit 1.

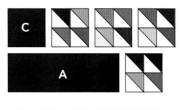
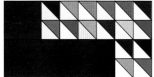
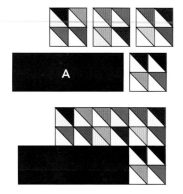

Unit 1 Diagrams

4. Join 4 Four Patch Units and 1 black print A rectangle as shown in *Unit 2 Diagrams*. Make 5 Unit 2.

Unit 2 Diagrams

5. Join 3 Four Patch Units, 1 black print A rectangle, and 1 black print C square as shown in *Unit 3 Diagrams*. Make 5 Unit 3.

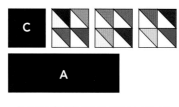
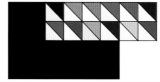

Unit 3 Diagrams

Quilt Assembly

1. Lay out Units 1, 2, and 3, black print B rectangles, and remaining black print C squares as shown in *Quilt Top Assembly Diagram*.
2. Join into diagonal rows; join rows.
3. Trim sides of quilt ¼" beyond points of outer Four Patch units as shown in

Quilt Top Assembly Diagram. Trim top and bottom of quilt ¼" beyond inner points as shown to complete quilt top.

Finishing

1. Divide backing into 2 (2⅝-yard) lengths. Cut 1 piece in half lengthwise to make 2 narrow panels. Join 1 narrow panel to each side of wider panel; press seam allowances toward narrow panels.
2. Layer backing, batting, and quilt top; baste. Quilt as desired. Quilt shown was hand quilted inside each triangle and with a feather design in background *(Quilting Diagram)*.
3. Join 2¼"-wide red print strips into 1 continuous piece for straight-grain French-fold binding. Add binding to quilt.

Quilt Top Assembly Diagram

Quilting Diagram

Scrappy Stars

This design has infinite possibilities. Pat Harrison used the same block unit arrangement to make two different quilts (see page 69). She changed only the block sashing and the fabrics to achieve two different looks.

PROJECT RATING: INTERMEDIATE

Size: 63" × 63"

Blocks: 16 (11") blocks

MATERIALS

4 yards total assorted medium/dark prints for blocks and outer border

¾ yard light green print for blocks

⅜ yard lime print for block center and sashing squares

¾ yard purple print for sashing

⅜ yard pink print for inner border

⅜ yard turquoise print for middle border

½ yard teal print for binding

4 yards backing fabric

Twin-size quilt batting

Cutting

Measurements include ¼" seam allowances.

From assorted medium/dark prints, cut a total of:

- 32 (5⅞") squares. Cut squares in half diagonally to make 64 half-square A triangles.
- 64 (3") C squares.
- 324 (1½" × 5½") D rectangles.

From light green print, cut:

- 6 (3⅜"-wide) strips. From strips, cut 64 (3⅜") squares. Cut squares in half diagonally to make 128 half-square B triangles.

From lime print, cut:

- 7 (1½"-wide) strips. From strips, cut 169 (1½") E squares.

From purple print, cut:

- 2 (11½"-wide) strips. From strips, cut 40 (11½" × 1½") sashing rectangles.

From pink print, cut:

- 7 (1½"-wide) strips. Piece strips to make 4 (1½" × 65½") inner border strips.

From turquoise print, cut:

- 7 (1½"-wide) strips. Piece strips to make 4 (1½" × 65½") middle border strips.

From teal print, cut:

- 7 (2¼"-wide) strips for binding.

Block Assembly

1. Join 1 dark print A triangle, 2 light green print B triangles, and 1 dark print C square as shown in *Block Unit Diagrams*. Make 4 Block Units.

Block Unit Diagrams

2. Referring to *Block Sashing Unit Diagrams*, place 1 lime print E square atop 1 dark print D rectangle, right sides facing. Stitch diagonally from corner to corner as shown. Trim ¼" beyond stitching. Press open to reveal triangle. Repeat for adjacent corner to complete 1 Block Sashing Unit. Make 4 Block Sashing Units.

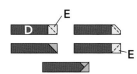

Block Sashing Unit Diagrams

3. Lay out Block Units, Block Sashing Units, and 1 lime print E square as shown in *Block Assembly Diagram*. Join into rows; join rows to complete 1 block *(Block Diagram)*. Make 16 blocks.

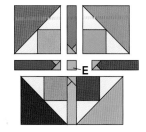

Block Assembly Diagram

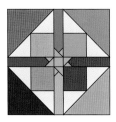

Block Diagram

Border Assembly

1. Join 65 dark print D rectangles as shown in *Border Diagram*. Add 1 turquoise print middle border strip and 1 pink print inner border strip to pieced rectangles to complete 1 pieced border.
2. Make 4 pieced borders.

Quilt Assembly

1. Lay out blocks, purple print sashing rectangles, and remaining lime print E squares as shown in *Quilt Top Assembly Diagram*.
2. Join into rows; join rows to complete quilt center.
3. Add borders to quilt center, mitering corners.

Web Extra

For instructions and a video on mitering borders, visit our Web site at: FonsandPorter.com/mborders.

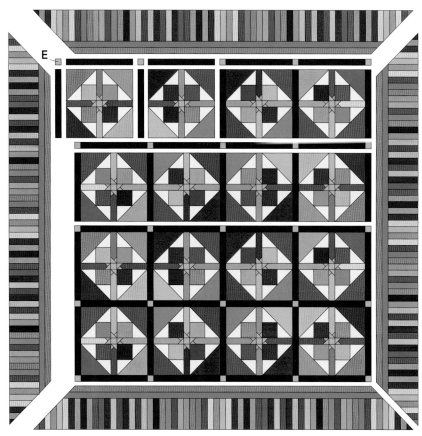

Quilt Top Assembly Diagram

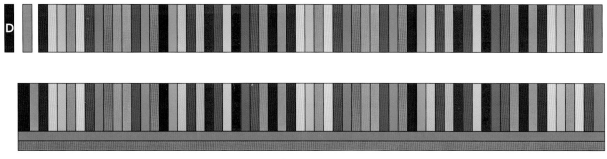

Border Diagrams

Finishing

1. Divide backing into 2 (2-yard lengths. Cut 1 piece in half lengthwise to make 2 narrow panels. Join 1 narrow panel to each side of wider panel; press seam allowances toward narrow panels.

2. Layer backing, batting, and quilt top; baste. Quilt as desired. Quilt shown was quilted in the ditch and with a petal design in blocks *(Quilting Diagram).*

3. Join 2¼"-wide teal print strips into 1 continuous piece for straight-grain French-fold binding. Add binding to quilt.

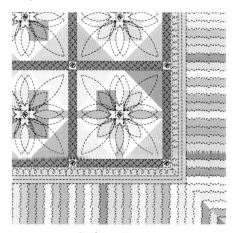

Quilting Diagram

DESIGNER

Pat Harrison has been obsessed with fabric and sewing for as long as she can remember. She discovered quilting after twenty years of teaching clothing construction, and hasn't stitched clothing since. Pat is an award-winning longarm quilter, and also designs quilts, teaches, lectures, and enjoys judging quilts.

SIZE OPTIONS

	Crib (39" × 51")	Full (75" × 99")
Blocks	6	35
Setting	2 × 3	5 × 7

MATERIALS

Assorted dark prints	2 yards	6½ yards
Light Green Print	1 fat quarter★	1⅜ yards
Lime Print	1 fat quarter★	¾ yard
Purple Print	⅜ yard	1½ yards
Pink Print	¼ yard	½ yard
Turquoise Print	¼ yard	½ yard
Binding Fabric	½ yard	¾ yard
Backing Fabric	1⅝ yards	6 yards
Batting	Crib-Size	Full-Size

★fat quarter = 18" × 20"

CRIB-SIZE Cutting

From assorted medium/dark prints, cut a total of:

- 12 (5⅞") squares. Cut squares in half diagonally to make 24 half-square A triangles.
- 24 (3") C squares.
- 204 (1½" × 5½") D rectangles.

From light green print fat quarter, cut:

- 5 (3⅜"-wide) strips. From strips, cut 24 (3⅜") squares. Cut squares in half diagonally to make 48 half-square B triangles.

From lime print fat quarter, cut:

- 6 (1½"-wide) strips. From strips, cut 66 (1½") E squares.

From purple print, cut:

- 1 (11½"-wide) strip. From strip, cut 17 (11½" × 1½") sashing rectangles.

From pink print, cut:

- 5 (1½"-wide) strips. From 2 strips, cut 2 (1½" × 39½") top and bottom inner border strips. Piece remaining strips to make 2 (1½" × 51½") side inner border strips.

From turquoise print, cut:

- 5 (1½"-wide) strips. From 2 strips, cut 2 (1½" × 39½") top and bottom middle border strips. Piece remaining strips to make 2 (1½" × 51½") side middle border strips.

From binding fabric, cut:

- 5 (2¼"-wide) strips for binding.

FULL-SIZE Cutting

From assorted medium/dark prints, cut a total of:

- 70 (5⅞") squares. Cut squares in half diagonally to make 140 half-square A triangles.
- 140 (3") C squares.
- 488 (1½" × 5½") D rectangles.

From light green print, cut:

- 13 (3⅜"-wide) strips. From strips, cut 140 (3⅜") squares. Cut squares in half diagonally to make 280 half-square B triangles.

From lime print, cut:

- 14 (1½"-wide) strips. From strips, cut 363 (1½") E squares.

From purple print, cut:

- 4 (11½"-wide) strips. From strips, cut 82 (11½" × 1½") sashing rectangles.

From pink print, cut:

- 10 (1½"-wide) strips. Piece strips to make 2 (1½" × 75½") top and bottom inner border strips and 2 (1½" × 99½") side inner border strips.

From turquoise print, cut:

- 10 (1½"-wide) strips. Piece strips to make 2 (1½" × 75½") top and bottom inner border strips and 2 (1½" × 99½") side inner border strips.

From binding fabric, cut:

- 10 (2¼"-wide) strips for binding.

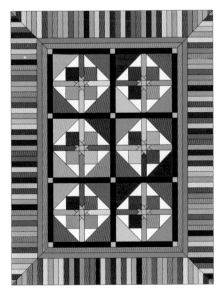

Crib-Size Diagram

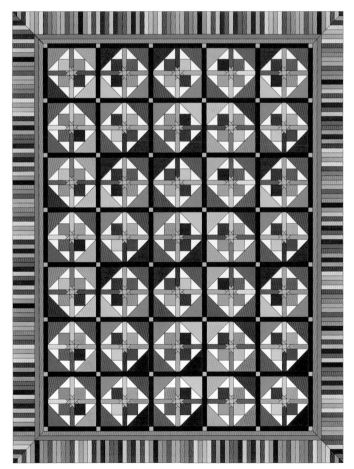

Full-Size Diagram

TRIED & TRUE

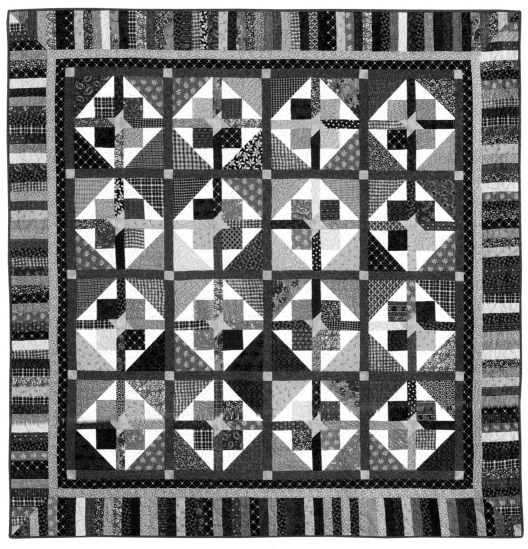

The second version of this quilt by Pat Harrison has gold Friendship Stars in the Block Sashing Units and E setting squares instead of lime Variable Stars as in the first version.

Cutting is the same except:

From gold print, cut:

• 5 (1½"-wide) strips. From strips, cut 105 (1½") E squares.

Block Assembly is the same except:

2. Referring to *Block Sashing Unit Diagrams*, place 1 gold print E square atop 1 dark print D rectangle, right sides facing. Stitch diagonally from corner to corner as shown. Trim ¼" beyond stitching. Press open to reveal triangle. Make 4 Block Sashing Units.

Scrappy Triangles

Jean Nolte's quilt began as a scrappy triangle-square exchange with a dozen friends. She used a teal batik for the sashing, borders, and binding to tie it all together.

PROJECT RATING: CHALLENGING

Size: 62" × 79"

Blocks: 12 (16") blocks

MATERIALS

18 fat quarters★★ or 36 fat eighths★ assorted dark prints

19 fat quarters★★ or 38 fat eighths★ assorted light prints

2¼ yards teal print for sashing, border, and binding

36 Laundry Basket Quilts Half-Square Triangle Exchange Papers (optional)

Fons & Porter Quarter Inch Seam Marker (optional)

4¾ yards backing fabric

Twin-size quilt batting

★fat eighth = 9" × 20"

★★fat quarter = 18" × 20"

Cutting

Measurements include ¼" seam allowances.

NOTE: Instructions are written using Half-Square Triangle Exchange Paper cut into smaller sections. This will make more combinations of prints for a scrappier look. See *Sew Easy: Quick Triangle-Squares* on page 79 for using the Fons & Porter Quarter Inch Seam Marker to make triangle-squares. If not using triangle papers or Quarter Inch Seam Marker, make 2" finished triangle-squares using your preferred method.

From assorted dark prints, cut a total of:

- 36 (6⅛"-wide) strips. From strips, cut 108 (6⅛") A squares.

From assorted light prints, cut a total of:

- 36 (6⅛"-wide) strips. From strips, cut 108 (6⅛") A squares.
- 18 (2½"-wide) strips. From strips, cut 144 (2½") B squares.
- 20 (1½") sashing squares.

From teal print, cut:

- 4 (2¼"-wide) **lengthwise** strips for binding.
- 13 (1½"-wide) **lengthwise** strips. From strips, 2 (1½" × 77½") side outer borders, 2 (1½" × 62½") top and bottom outer borders, 31 (1½" × 16½") long sashing strips, and 18 (1½" × 4½") short sashing strips.

Triangle-Squares

1. Cut triangle papers into 108 sections of 4 squares each. Layer 1 light print A square atop 1 dark print A square, right sides facing. Place 1 paper square atop pair of squares; pin in place.

> ### Sew Smart™
>
> Seam allowance of the triangle-squares will all automatically go toward the dark fabric when pressed if the paper is placed on the light fabric.—Liz

2. Stitch on dashed lines as shown in *Stitching Diagram*. Cut on all solid lines, including outer lines, to make 8 triangle-squares. With paper still attached, press seam allowances of triangle-squares toward dark fabric. Repeat to make a total of 864 triangle-squares. Carefully remove paper from triangle-squares.

Stitching Diagram

Block Assembly

1. Lay out 13 triangle-squares and 3 light print B squares as shown in *Quadrant Diagram*. Join into rows; join rows to complete 1 quadrant. Make 4 quadrants.

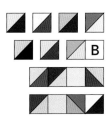

Quadrant Diagram

2. Lay out 4 quadrants as shown in *Block Assembly Diagram*. Join into rows, join rows to complete 1 block (*Block Diagram*). Make 12 blocks.

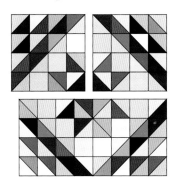

Block Assembly Diagram

Block Diagram

Border Unit Assembly

1. Lay out 16 triangle-squares as shown in *Border Unit Assembly Diagram*. Join into rows; join rows to complete 1 Border Unit (*Border Unit Diagram*). Make 14 Border Units.

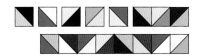

Border Unit Assembly Diagram

Border Unit Diagram

2. Lay out 4 triangle-squares as shown in *Corner Unit Assembly Diagram*. Join into rows; join rows to complete 1 Corner Unit (*Corner Unit Diagram*). Make 4 Corner Units.

Corner Unit Assembly Diagram

Corner Unit Diagram

Quilt Assembly

1. Lay out blocks, sashing strips, sashing squares, Border Units, and Corner Units as shown in *Quilt Top Assembly Diagram*.
2. Join into rows; join rows to complete quilt center.
3. Add teal print side outer borders to quilt center. Add top and bottom outer borders to quilt.

Finishing

1. Divide backing into 2 (2⅜-yard) lengths. Cut 1 piece in half lengthwise to make 2 narrow panels. Join 1 narrow panel to each side of wider panel. Press seam allowances toward narrow panels.
2. Layer backing, batting, and quilt top; baste. Quilt as desired. Quilt shown was quilted in the ditch and with a diamond in the background of the stars (*Quilting Diagram*).
3. Join 2¼"-wide teal print strips into 1 continuous piece for straight-grain French-fold binding. Add binding to quilt.

Quilting Diagram

Quilt Top Assembly Diagram

DESIGNER

Jean Nolte is the Editor of all the Fons & Porter magazines, and is also the Editorial Director of "Love of Quilting" on public television. She has been quilting for nearly thirty years, and is always excited to try a new technique. Her fabric stash contains more yardage than she could possibly use in a lifetime, but she is having lots of fun trying. When not quilting, Jean loves to travel, knit, or spend time with her family.

Texas Two Step

Make this easy quilt using a great bundle of fat quarters or fabrics from your stash.
Choose two or three color families for a more controlled look or throw
everything in for a super-scrappy quilt.

PROJECT RATING: EASY

Size: 67½" × 82½"

Blocks: 32 (7½") Old Maid's Puzzle blocks

31 (7½") Hourglass blocks

MATERIALS

32 fat quarters★ assorted prints in brown, red, and blue

Fons & Porter Quarter Inch Seam Marker (optional)

5 yards backing fabric

Twin-size quilt batting

★fat quarter = 18" × 20"

Cutting

Measurements include ¼" seam allowances. Instructions are written for using the Fons & Porter Quarter Inch Seam Marker. If not using this ruler, follow cutting **NOTES.**

From assorted print fat quarters, cut a total of:

• 16 (8¾"-wide) strips. From strips, cut 31 (8¾") squares. Cut squares in half diagonally in both directions to make 124 quarter-square triangles.

NOTE: Cut the following A and B squares in 32 matching sets of 3 A squares and 3 B squares, and 32 matching sets of 3 A squares.

• 20 (3⅜"-wide) strips. From strips, cut 96 (3⅜") A squares.

NOTE: If not using the Fons & Porter Quarter Inch Seam Marker, cut the 3⅜" squares in half diagonally to make 192 half-square triangles.

• 64 (3"-wide) strips. From 16 strips, cut 96 (3") B squares. Remaining strips are for borders. Cut each remaining strip into 2 or 3 pieces of various lengths for borders.

• 20 (2¼"-wide) strips for binding.

Block Assembly

1. Referring to *Sew Easy: Quick Triangle-Squares* on page 79, make 6 matching triangle-squares using 3 matching dark print A squares and 3 matching light print A squares.

NOTE: If not using the Fons & Porter Quarter Inch Seam Marker, join 2 half-square triangles as shown in *Triangle-Square Diagrams*. Make 6 matching triangle-squares.

Triangle-Square Diagrams

2. Lay out triangle-squares and 3 matching B squares as shown in *Old Maid's Puzzle Block Assembly Diagram*. Join into rows; join rows to complete 1 Old Maid's Puzzle block (*Old Maid's Puzzle Block Diagram*). Make 32 Old Maid's Puzzle blocks.

Old Maid's Puzzle
Block Assembly Diagram

Old Maid's Puzzle Block Diagram

3. Join 4 quarter-square triangles as shown in *Hourglass Block Diagrams*. Make 31 Hourglass blocks.

Hourglass Block Diagrams

Quilt Assembly

1. Lay out blocks as shown in *Quilt Top Assembly Diagram*.

2. Join blocks into rows; join rows to complete quilt center.

3. Measure length of quilt. Join assorted border strips to make 1 side inner border this measurement. Make 2 side inner borders. Add borders to quilt center.

Quilt Top Assembly Diagram

4. Measure width of quilt, including borders. Join assorted border strips to make 1 top inner border this measurement. Repeat for bottom inner border. Add borders to quilt.

Sew Smart™
Choose strips from the same fabrics for ends of borders to make borders match at corners.
—Marianne

5. Repeat for middle and outer borders.

Finishing

1. Divide backing into 2 (2½-yard) lengths. Divide 1 piece in half lengthwise to make 2 narrow panels. Add 1 narrow panel to each side of wider panel. Press seam allowances toward narrow panels.

2. Layer backing, batting, and quilt top; baste. Quilt as desired. Quilt shown was quilted with a clamshell design (*Quilting Diagram*).

3. Join 2¼"-wide assorted print strips into 1 continuous piece for straight-grain French-fold binding. Add binding to quilt.

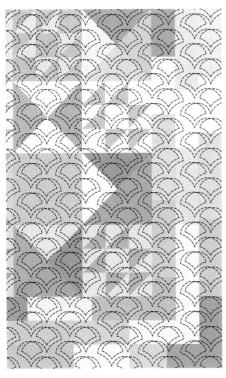

Quilting Diagram

SIZE OPTIONS

	Throw (60" × 75")	Full (82½" × 97½")
Old Maid's Puzzle Blocks	24	50
Hourglass Blocks	24	49
Setting	6 × 8	9 × 11

MATERIALS

Assorted Prints	26 fat quarters	55 fat quarters
Backing Fabric	3¾ yards	7½ yards
Batting	Twin-Size	Queen-Size

Web **Extra**

Go to FonsandPorter.com/ttwostepsizes to download Quilt Top Assembly Diagrams and cutting instructions for these size options.

TRIED & TRUE

We used prints from the Punch Paisley collection by Punch Studio for Hoffman Fabrics for a contemporary version of this design.

DESIGNER

Jane Vaughan began quilting in 1993. In 2007, she was given the opportunity to design a mystery quilt for Mill House Quilts in Waunakee, Wisconsin. Since that time she has designed more than thirty mystery quilts and patterns under the Thornberry Quilts name. She teaches classes and is president of the Mad City Quilt Guild in Madison, Wisconsin.

Sew Easy™

Quick Triangle-Squares

Use this quick method to make the triangle-squares for *Scrappy Triangles*
on page 70, *Texas Two Step* on page 74, and *Scrapbook* on page 80.
The Fons & Porter Quarter Inch Seam Marker offers a neat
way to mark accurate sewing lines for this method.

1. From each of 2 fabrics, cut 1 square ⅞" larger than the desired finished size of
   the triangle-square. For example, to make a triangle-square that will finish 2", as
   in the *Scrappy Triangles* quilt on page 70 or *Scrapbook* quilt on page 80, cut 2⅞"
   squares.

2. On wrong side of lighter square, place the Quarter Inch Seam Marker diagonally
   across the square, with the yellow center line positioned exactly at opposite
   corners. Mark stitching lines along both sides of the Quarter Inch Seam Marker
   (*Photo A*).

   NOTE: If you are not using the Fons & Porter Quarter Inch Seam Marker, draw a
   diagonal line from corner to corner across square. Then draw sewing lines on each
   side of the first line, ¼" away.

3. Place light square atop darker square, right sides facing; stitch along both marked
   sewing lines.

4. Cut between rows of stitching to make 2 triangle-squares (*Photo B*).

QUILT BY **Christina McCourt**.

MACHINE QUILTED BY **Gina Janes**.

Scrapbook

Make a scrappy full-size bed quilt using authentic reproduction fabrics.
Use the Fons & Porter Quarter Inch Seam Marker and our Sew Easy lesson
on page 79 to make the triangle-squares.

PROJECT RATING: INTERMEDIATE

Size: 82" × 94"

Blocks: 36 (10") blocks

MATERIALS

24 fat quarters★ assorted medium/
   dark prints for blocks

2¼ yards tan solid for blocks

1⅝ yards red solid for inner border
   and binding

1¾ yards blue print for outer border

Fons & Porter Quarter Inch Seam
   Marker (optional)

7½ yards backing fabric

Queen-size quilt batting

★fat quarter = 18" × 20"

Cutting

Measurements include ¼" seam allowances. Border strips are exact length needed. You may want to make them longer to allow for piecing variations. Instructions are written for using the Fons & Porter Quarter Inch Seam Marker. If not using this ruler, follow cutting **NOTES**.

From assorted dark print fat quarters, cut a total of:

• 144 (2⅞") squares.
   NOTE: If not using the Fons & Porter Quarter Inch Seam Marker, cut squares in half diagonally to make 288 half-square A triangles.

• 36 (2½" × 10½") E rectangles.

• 72 (2½" × 6½") D rectangles.

• 72 (2½" × 4½") C rectangles.

• 138 (2½") B squares.

From tan solid, cut:

• 12 (2⅞"-wide) strips. From strips, cut 144 (2⅞") squares.
   NOTE: If not using the Fons & Porter Quarter Inch Seam Marker, cut squares in half diagonally to make 288 half-square A triangles.

• 16 (2½"-wide) strips. From strips, cut 255 (2½") B squares.

From red solid, cut:

• 12 (2½"-wide) strips. Piece strips to make 2 (2½" × 78½") side inner borders, 2 (2½" × 70½") top and bottom inner borders, and 2 (2½" × 66½") F rectangles.

• 10 (2¼"-wide) strips for binding.

From blue print, cut:

• 9 (6½"-wide) strips. Piece strips to make 4 (6½" × 82½") outer borders.

Block Assembly

1. Referring to *Sew Easy: Quick Triangle-Squares* on page 79, make 288 triangle-squares using tan and dark print (2⅞") squares.
   NOTE: If not using the Fons & Porter Quarter Inch Seam Marker, join 1 dark print A triangle and 1 tan A triangle to make a triangle-square (*Triangle-Square Diagrams*). Make 288 triangle-squares.

Triangle-Square Diagrams

2. Lay out 8 triangle-squares, 5 tan B squares, 2 dark print B squares, 2 dark print C rectangles, and 2 dark print D rectangles as shown in *Block Assembly Diagrams*. Join into sections; join sections to complete 1 block *(Block Diagram)*. Make 36 blocks.

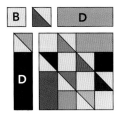

Block Assembly Diagrams

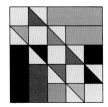

Block Diagram

Quilt Assembly

1. Lay out blocks, dark print E rect-angles, and 9 tan B squares as shown in *Quilt Top Assembly Diagram*.
2. Join into rows; join rows to complete quilt center.

Quilt Top Assembly Diagram

3. Join 33 dark print B squares, 33 tan B squares, and 1 red F rectangle to complete 1 Border Unit. Make 2 Border Units.
4. Add Border Units to top and bottom of quilt center.
5. Add red side inner borders to quilt center. Add red top and bottom inner borders to quilt.
6. Repeat for blue print outer borders.

Finishing

1. Divide backing into 3 (2½-yard) lengths. Join panels lengthwise. Seams will run horizontally.
2. Layer backing, batting, and quilt top; baste. Quilt as desired. Quilt shown was quilted with continuous curves in blocks, scroll designs in blocks and inner border, and meandering in outer border *(Quilting Diagram)*.
3. Join 2¼"-wide red strips into 1 continuous piece for straight-grain French-fold binding. Add binding to quilt.

Quilting Diagram

DESIGNER

Christina McCourt started quilting in 2001, and began designing her own quilts in 2008. She has four children, and lives in New London, Missouri. In addition to designing quilts, she is a substitute school teacher.

TRIED & TRUE

Assorted reproduction 1930s fabrics give this design a different vintage look. Solids form a diagonal grid to separate the prints.

Tossed Greens

Designer Pam Peck came up with an innovative way to use the green fabrics in her collection. Look through your stash and choose fabrics in your favorite color to make this scrappy log cabin variation.

PROJECT RATING: EASY

Size: 55" × 55"

Blocks: 25 (11") Log Cabin blocks

MATERIALS

16 fat quarters★ assorted green prints for blocks. (For an even scrappier look, use more fabrics.)

½ yard dark green print for binding

3½ yards backing fabric

Twin-size quilt batting

★fat quarter = 18" × 20"

Cutting

Measurements include ¼" seam allowances.

From each fat quarter, cut:

- 13 (1½" × 18") **lengthwise** strips. From 1 strip, cut 4 (1½") squares for block centers. (You will have a few extra.)

From dark green print, cut:

- 6 (2¼"-wide) strips for binding.

Sew Smart™

This quilt is a fantastic way to use up scraps in your stash. Cut 1½"-wide strips from your leftover fabrics and then piece random lengths together using diagonal seams. The logs for your Log Cabin blocks will be unique! —Marianne

Block Assembly

1. With right sides facing, join two (1½") squares for Block Center Unit. Repeat to make 25 Block Center Units.

2. Join batches of 5 or 6 strips randomly as shown in *Diagonal Seams Diagrams*. Stitch diagonally across strips. Trim ¼" beyond stitching. Press open to make 1 continuous strip.

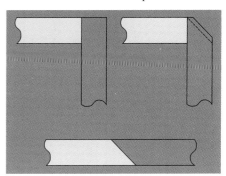

Diagonal Seams Diagrams

3. Referring to *Piece #3 Diagrams*, position right edge of one Block Center Unit atop 1 (1½"-wide) strip with right sides facing. Stitch Block Center Unit to strip. Press; trim excess strip even with bottom edge of Block Center Unit.

Block Center Unit

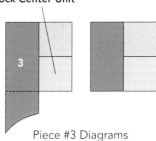

Piece #3 Diagrams

4. Referring to *Piece #4 Diagrams*, stitch strip to center as shown. Open out strip, press, and trim excess strip even with piece #3.

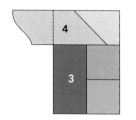 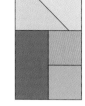

Piece #4 Diagrams

5. Continue to add pieces in numerical order, working clockwise, to complete 1 block *(Block Diagram)*. Make 25 Log Cabin blocks.

Quilt Assembly

1. Lay out blocks as shown in *Quilt Top Assembly Diagram*.

2. Join into horizontal rows; join rows to complete quilt top.

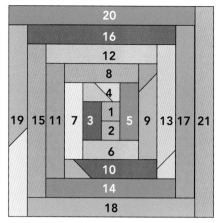

Block Diagram

Quilt Top Assembly Diagram

Finishing

1. Divide backing fabric into 2 (1¾-yard) pieces. Cut one piece in half lengthwise to make 2 narrow panels. Join 1 narrow panel to wider panel; press seam allowances toward narrow panel. Remaining panel is extra and may be used to make a hanging sleeve.

2. Layer backing, batting, and quilt top; baste. Quilt as desired. Quilt shown was stitched in the ditch.

3. Join 2¼"-wide dark green print strips into 1 continuous piece for straight-grain French-fold binding. Add binding to quilt.

TRIED & TRUE

We made this scrappy Log Cabin block in a variety of blue prints from our own fabric stash.

DESIGNER

Pam Peck started quilting twenty-three years ago as an escape from the stresses of daily life. Short on time, yet full of creativity, she developed a unique method of using her stash of fat quarters to make quick, scrappy quilts. Now retired, she looks forward to spending more time quilting and developing new techniques.

Simply Squares

Send a high school graduate off to college with a perfect brightener for her dormitory room. Let the fabric do the work for you by choosing her favorite colors and cutting big squares.

PROJECT RATING: EASY

Size: 68¼" × 84"

MATERIALS

24 fat quarters★ assorted prints and plaids
¾ yard pink print for binding
5½ yards backing fabric
Full-size quilt batting
★fat quarter = 18" × 20"

Cutting

Measurements include ¼" seam allowances.

From each fat quarter, cut:

- 3 (5¾"-wide) strips. From strips, cut 9 (5¾") squares.

From pink print, cut:

- 9 (2¼"-wide) strips for binding.

Quilt Assembly

1. Referring to photo on page 90, lay out squares in 16 rows of 13 squares each.

2. Join squares into rows; join rows to complete quilt top.

Finishing

1. Divide backing fabric into 2 (2¾-yard) pieces. Cut 1 piece in half length-wise to make 2 narrow panels. Join 1 narrow panel to each side of wider panel. Press seam allowances toward narrow panels.

2. Layer backing, batting, and quilt top; baste. Quilt as desired. Quilt shown was quilted with an overall daisy and leaf design (*Quilting Diagram*).

3. Join 2¼"-wide pink print strips into 1 continuous piece for straight-grain French-fold binding. Add binding to quilt.

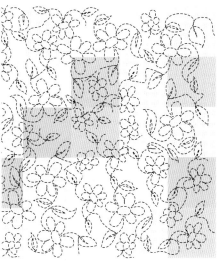

Quilting Diagram

SIZE OPTIONS

	Crib (36¾" × 47¼")	Full (84" × 94½")
Squares	63	288
Setting	7 × 9	16 × 18

MATERIALS

Assorted prints	7 fat quarters★	32 fat quarters★
Pink Print	½ yard	¾ yard
Backing Fabric	1½ yards	7½ yards
Batting	Crib-Size	Queen-Size

★fat quarter = 18" × 20"

Web Extra

Go to FonsandPorter.com/squaresizes to download Quilt Top Assembly Diagrams for these size options.

TRIED & TRUE

Simple squares of fun, juvenile prints make a perfect quick-to-make quilt for a younger recipient.

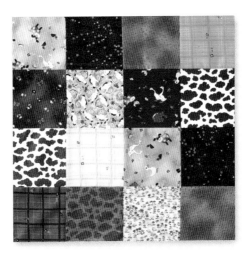

1930s Re-Bloom

This treasure of bright blue, yellow, pink, peach, lavender, and mint green is a reproduction of a much-loved quilt made in the 1930s, by Mary Ocker's great-aunt.

PROJECT RATING: INTERMEDIATE
Size: 44" × 56"
Blocks: 12 (10") blocks

MATERIALS

12 fat eighths★ assorted 1930s prints for appliqués
6 fat eighths★ assorted 1930s solids for appliqués
1¼ yards cream solid for block backgrounds
1¼ yards green solid for sashing and border
½ yard green print for binding
Paper-backed fusible web
3 yards backing fabric
Twin-size quilt batting
★fat eighth = 9" × 20"

Cutting

Measurements include ¼" seam allowances. Border strips are exact length needed. You may want to make them longer to allow for piecing variations. Pattern for Petal is on page 94. Follow manufacturer's instructions if using fusible web.

NOTE: Instructions for needle-turn appliqué are in *Sew Easy: Needle-turn Appliqué* on page 95.

From each print fat eighth, cut:
• 8 Petals.
From each solid fat eighth, cut:
• 8 Petals.
From cream solid, cut:
• 4 (10½"-wide) strips. From strips, cut 12 (10½") block background squares.
From green solid, cut:
• 5 (5½"-wide) strips. Piece strips to make 2 (5½" × 44½") top and bottom borders and 2 (5½" × 46½") side borders.
• 6 (2½"-wide) strips. From strips, cut 3 (2½" × 34½") horizontal sashing rectangles and 8 (2½" × 10½") vertical sashing rectangles.
From green print, cut:
• 6 (2¼"-wide) strips for binding.

Block Assembly

1. Arrange 4 matching solid petals and 8 matching print petals atop 1 cream block background square as shown in *Block Diagram*.

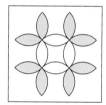

Block Diagram

2. Appliqué pieces in place to complete 1 block. Make 12 blocks.

Quilt Assembly

1. Lay out blocks, vertical sashing rectangles, and horizontal sashing rectangles as shown in *Quilt Top Assembly Diagram* on page 94. Join into rows; join rows to complete quilt center.

2. Add green side borders to quilt center. Add top and bottom borders to quilt.

Finishing

1. Divide backing into 2 (1½-yard) lengths. Join panels lengthwise. Seam will run horizontally.

2. Layer backing, batting, and quilt top; baste. Quilt as desired. Quilt shown was outline quilted around the appliqué pieces and has a diamond design in the sashing and a diagonal grid in the borders *(Quilting Diagram)*.

3. Join 2¼"-wide green print strips into 1 continuous piece for straight-grain French-fold binding. Add binding to quilt.

Quilting Diagram

DESIGNER

Mary Ocker started quilting about a year ago. She had the original quilt of this same design, which was made by her great-aunt Hazel in the 1930s. Since it was worn and faded, Mary decided to make a new one using 1930s reproduction fabrics.

Quilt Top Assembly Diagram

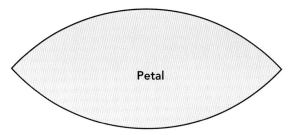

Petal

Pattern is shown full size for use with fusible web. Add ³/₁₆" seam allowance for hand appliqué.

Needle-Turn Appliqué

Needle-turn appliqué derives its name from the action of turning under the seam allowance edge of appliqué pieces with the needle used for stitching. Use a blindstitch to secure the folded edge of fabric to a background.

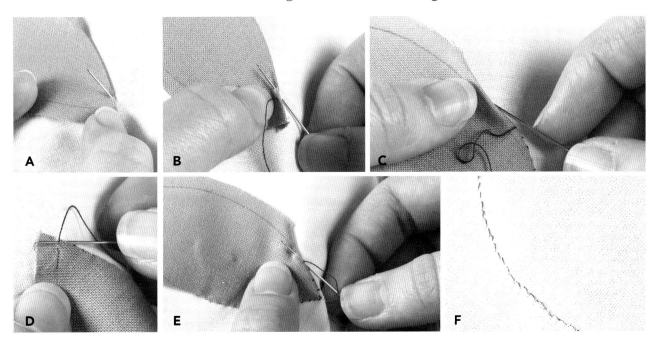

A

B

C

D

E

F

Sew Smart™
Use thread to match your appliqué piece. Photos show stitching with contrasting thread for visibility.
—Marianne

1. Pull needle and knotted thread up through background fabric and folded edge of appliqué piece, barely catching edge of fold (*Photo A*).

2. Reinsert needle into background fabric beside folded edge where thread was first brought through, and make a ⅛" stitch, bringing point of needle back up through background fabric and through folded edge of appliqué piece (*Photo B*).

   NOTE: As you begin each stitch, make sure needle enters background fabric right next to thread coming up through folded edge of appliqué.

3. Use point of needle to turn under a small portion of the appliqué piece seam allowance, using needle to smooth curves in folded edge (*Photo C*).

4. Stitch to outer points, take a small extra stitch directly at the point. Use needle to turn seam allowance under on other side of point and continue stitching (*Photos D and E*).

Sew Smart™
Pull each stitch to keep it tight, but do not pucker background fabric.
—Marianne

Stitches on top should be nearly invisible. Stitches on back side of background fabric should be straight and approximately ⅛" long (*Photo F*).

QUILT DESIGNED BY **Brandi Frey.**
MADE BY **Bev Getschel.**

Tangerine Zoo

Make this sweet crib quilt for your favorite youngster.
You'll be amazed at how easy it is to make the Dresden plate wedges.

PROJECT RATING: EASY

Size: 44" × 44"

Blocks: 9 (12") Dresden Plate blocks

MATERIALS

1 yard orange print for block centers and border

1¼ yards white print for block backgrounds

½ yard orange solid for binding

10 fat quarters★ assorted prints and solids in orange, lavender, yellow, and green for blocks

Template material

3 yards backing fabric

Crib-size quilt batting

★fat quarter = 18" × 20"

Cutting

Measurements include ¼" seam allowances. Border strips are exact length needed. You may want to cut them longer to allow for piecing variations. Patterns for Wedge and Circle are on page 100.

From orange print, cut:

- 4 (4½"-wide) strips. From strips, cut 4 (4½" × 36½") borders.
- 9 Circles, centering 1 printed animal in each, if desired.

From white print, cut:

- 3 (12½"-wide) strips. From strips, cut 9 (12½") A squares.
- 1 (4½"-wide) strip. From strip, cut 4 (4½") B squares.

From orange solid, cut:

- 5 (2¼"-wide) strips for binding.

From each fat quarter, cut:

- 9 Wedges.

Block Assembly

1. Fold 1 Wedge in half lengthwise, right sides facing. Stitch across top as shown in *Stitching Diagram.* Trim corner.

Stitching Diagram   Wedge Diagram

2. Open seam and turn point right side out. Press, centering seam as shown in *Wedge Diagram.* Make 90 Wedges.

3. Join 10 Wedges as shown in *Plate Diagram.* Make 9 Plates.

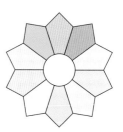

Plate Diagram

4. Center 1 Plate and 1 orange print Circle atop 1 white print A square. Pin in place. Machine appliqué points of plate using matching thread.

5. Baste plate to square ⅛" from edge of inner circle. Turn under seam allowance as you appliqué Circle in place to complete 1 block *(Block Diagram)*. Make 9 blocks.

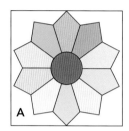

Block Diagram

Quilt Assembly

1. Lay out blocks as shown in *Quilt Top Assembly Diagram*. Join into rows; join rows to complete quilt center.

2. Add 1 orange print side border to each side of quilt center.

3. Add 1 white print B square to each end of remaining borders. Add borders to top and bottom of quilt.

Finishing

1. Divide backing into 2 (1½-yard) lengths. Cut 1 piece in half lengthwise to make 2 narrow panels. Join 1 narrow panel to wider panel. Remaining panel is extra and can be used to make a hanging sleeve.

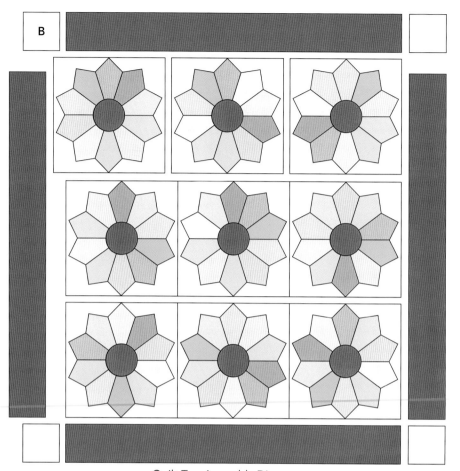

Quilt Top Assembly Diagram

2. Layer backing, batting, and quilt top; baste. Quilt as desired. Quilt shown was quilted with continuous curves in each plate and overall meandering in block backgrounds. Borders were quilted with a flower and leaf design *(Quilting Diagram)*.

3. Join 2¼"-wide orange strips into 1 continuous piece for straight-grain French-fold binding. Add binding to quilt.

Quilting Assembly Diagram

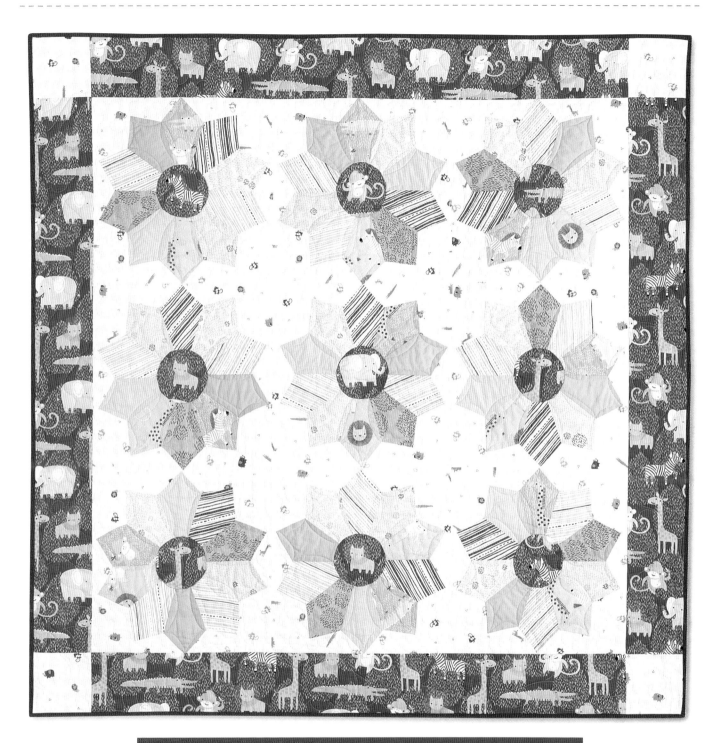

DESIGNER

Brandi Frey found her love of quilting in college, and has been quilting and sewing ever since. She and her family live in Seattle, Washington.

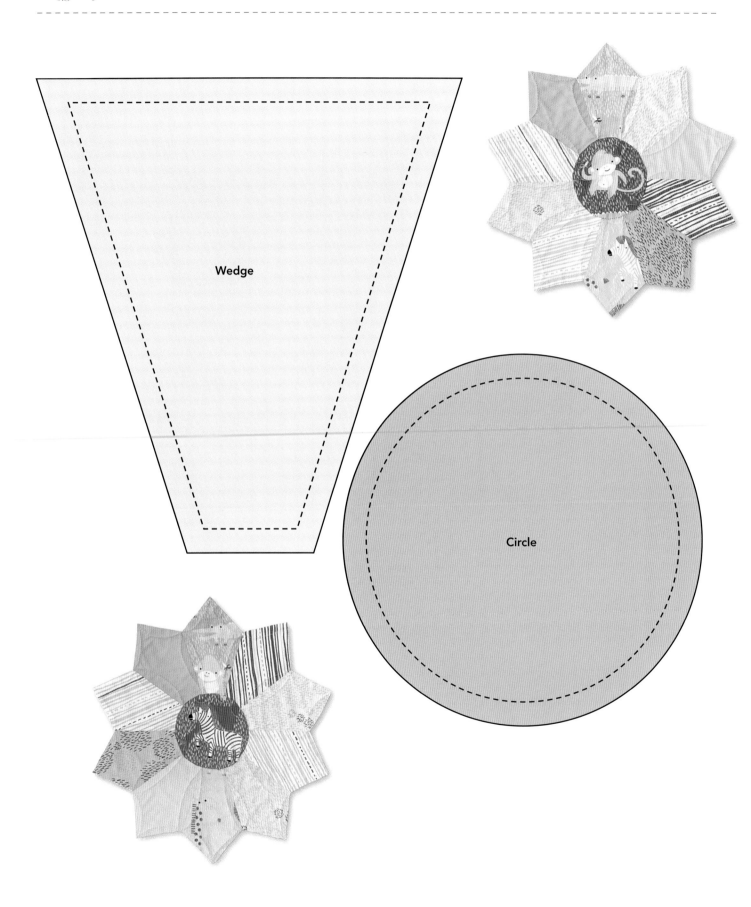

Wedge

Circle

SIZE OPTIONS

	Twin (68" × 92")
Blocks	35
Setting	5 × 7

MATERIALS

Orange Print	1½ yards
White Print	4½ yards
Orange Solid	¾ yard
10 Assorted Prints	¾ yard each
Backing Fabric	5½ yards
Batting	Queen-Size

Web **Extra**

Go to FonsandPorter.com/tangerinesizes to download Quilt Top Assembly Diagram for this size option.

TRIED & TRUE

Make a traditional version of the Dresden Plate block using reproduction prints in brown and green. These fabrics are from Jo Morton's Elizabethtown collection by Andover Fabrics. We machine appliquéd the plate to the background using invisible thread.

Zig and Zag

This quilt was designed by Evelyn Young as a National Quilting Day project for her guild. Make it with lots of fabrics for a scrappy look, or just a few for a more subtle design.

PROJECT RATING: EASY

Size: 34" × 45"

MATERIALS

6 fat quarters★ assorted prints in yellow, pink, green, blue, and lavender

1 yard white solid

½ yard light blue print for setting triangles

Fons & Porter Easy Diagonal Sets Ruler (optional)

1½ yards backing fabric

Crib-size quilt batting

★fat quarter = 18" × 20"

Cutting

Measurements include ¼" seam allowances. Instructions are written for using the Fons & Porter Easy Diagonal Sets Ruler. For instructions on using this ruler, go to FonsandPorter.com/SettingTriangles. If not using this ruler, follow cutting **NOTE**.

From assorted fat quarters, cut a total of:

• 22 (2½"-wide) strips for strip sets.
• 10 (2¼"-wide) strips for binding.

From white solid, cut:

• 11 (2½"-wide) strips. Cut strips in half to make 22 (2½" × 20") strips for strip sets for strip sets.

From light blue print, cut:

• 3 (3⅞"-wide) strips. From strips, cut 20 side setting triangles and 4 corner setting triangles.

NOTE: If not using the Fons & Porter Easy Diagonal Sets Ruler, cut 1 (7"-wide) strip and 1 (6⅝"-wide) strip.

From 7"-wide strip, cut 5 (7") squares. Cut squares in half diagonally in both directions to make 20 side setting triangles. From 6⅝"-wide strip, cut 2 (6⅝") squares. Cut squares in half diagonally to make 4 corner setting triangles.

Strip Set Assembly

1. Join 1 print strip and 1 white strip as shown in *Strip Set Diagram*. Make 22 strip sets.

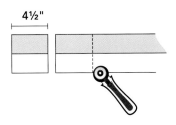

Strip Set Diagram

2. From strip sets, cut 82 (4½"-wide) segments.

Quilt Assembly

1. Lay out segments and setting triangles as shown in *Quilt Top Assembly Diagram*.

2. Join into diagonal rows; join rows to complete quilt top.

Finishing

1. Layer backing, batting, and quilt top; baste. Quilt as desired. Quilt shown was quilted in the ditch and with wavy lines in zigzags *(Quilting Diagram)*.

2. Join 2¼"-wide assorted print strips into 1 continuous piece for straight-grain French-fold binding. Add binding to quilt.

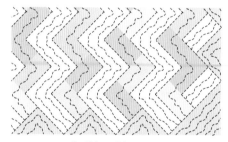

Quilting Diagram

Quilt Top Assembly Diagram

SIZE OPTIONS

	Throw (56½" × 73½")	Twin (68" × 85")	Full (79" × 90½")
Strip Sets	60	84	106
Segments	237	333	418

MATERIALS

Assorted Prints	12 fat quarters★	16 fat quarters★	20 fat quarters★
White Solid	2⅛ yards	3⅛ yards	3⅞ yards
Light Blue Print	¾ yard	¾ yards	¾ yards
Backing Fabric	3½ yards	5 yards	7½ yards
Batting	Twin-Size	Twin-Size	Full-Size

★Fat quarter = 18" × 20"

Web **Extra**

Go to FonsandPorter.com/zigandzagsizes to download Quilt Top Assembly Diagrams and cutting instructions for these size options.

TRIED & TRUE

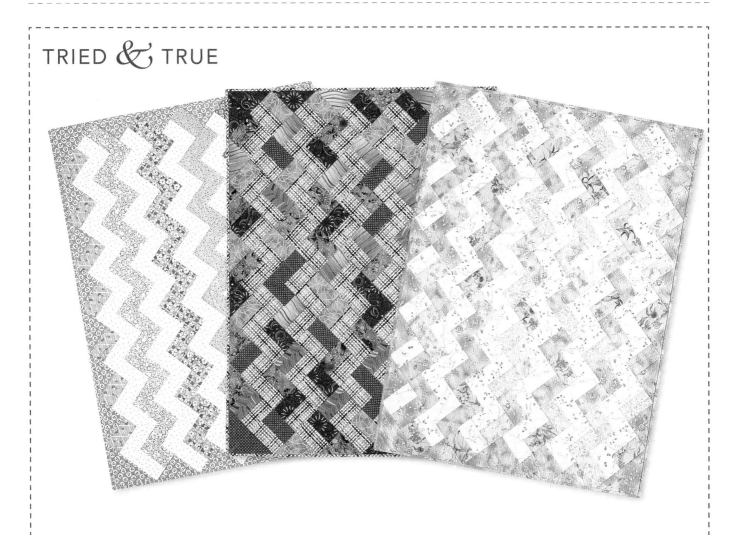

Experiment with fabric placement to achieve many different looks from this pattern.
Here are three more quilts Evelyn made.

DESIGNER

Evelyn Young collects fabrics that she loves. When ready to start a new project, she "shops" in her stash. She is inspired by fabric, and loves to use a variety of prints in her quilts.

QUILT DESIGNED AND MACHINE QUILTED BY **Sally Weber**.
MADE BY **QFK Sewing Group** under Barbara Beraney.

Pixie Sticks

The blocks in this quilt are so easy to make! Use randomly cut strips, and stitch them to a muslin foundation—no fussy piecing, no matching seams, and no worry about the blocks being the wrong size!

PROJECT RATING: EASY

Size: 42" × 54½"

Blocks: 12 (11") blocks

MATERIALS

1⅜ yards muslin for foundations

1 fat quarter★ black print #1 for block centers

¼ yard each of 12 assorted bright prints

1¼ yards black print for sashing, border, and binding

2¾ yards backing fabric

Crib-size quilt batting

★fat quarter = 18" × 20"

Cutting

Measurements include ¼" seam allowances. Border strips are exact length needed. You may want to make them longer to allow for piecing variations.

From muslin, cut:

- 4 (11½"-wide) strips. From strips, cut 12 (11½") foundation squares.

From black print #1 fat quarter, cut:

- 12 randomly-cut triangles of various sizes, centering motif in each.

From assorted bright prints, cut:

- 40"-long strips of various widths from 1" to 2½".

From black print #2, cut:

- 5 (3½"-wide) strips. Piece strips to make 2 (3½" × 49") side borders and 2 (3½" × 42½") top and bottom borders.
- 5 (2¼"-wide) strips for binding.
- 6 (2"-wide) strips. From strips, cut 3 (2" × 36½") horizontal sashing strips and 8 (2" × 11½") vertical sashing strips.

Quilt Assembly

1. Make 12 blocks as described in *Sew Easy: Crazy Pieced Blocks* on page 111.
2. Lay out blocks and sashing strips as shown in *Quilt Top Assembly Diagram* on page 108.
3. Join blocks and vertical sashing strips into rows; join rows and horizontal sashing strips to complete quilt center.
4. Add black print side borders to quilt center. Add top and bottom borders to quilt.

Quilt Top Assembly Diagram

Finishing

1. Divide backing into 2 (1⅜-yard) pieces. Cut 1 piece in half length-wise to make 2 narrow panels. Join 1 narrow panel to wider panel; press seam allowance toward narrow panel. Remaining panel is extra and can be used to make a hanging sleeve.

2. Layer backing, batting, and quilt top; baste. Quilt as desired. Quilt shown was quilted with meandering loops (*Quilting Diagram*).

3. Join 2¼"-wide black print strips into 1 continuous piece for straight-grain French-fold binding. Add binding to quilt.

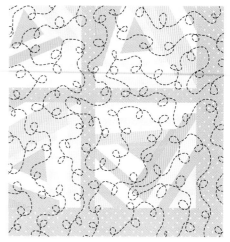

Quilting Diagram

TRIED & TRUE

We made our scrappy block with kids' prints from the Starlight Flannel collection by Blank Quilting.

DESIGNER

Sally Weber began sewing as a young child, and gradually worked into garment making. She learned to quilt after the birth of her first child. Sally is the Chapter Coordinator for Quilts for Kids.

SIZE OPTIONS

	Throw (54½" × 79½")	Twin (67" × 92")	Full (79½" × 92")
Blocks	24	35	42
Setting	4 × 6	5 × 7	6 × 7

MATERIALS

Muslin	2⅝ yards	4 yards	4¾ yards
Black Print #1	½ yard	⅞ yard	1 yard
Assorted Bright Prints	24 (¼-yard) pieces	35 (¼-yard) pieces	42 (¼-yard) pieces
Black Print #2	¾ yard	⅞ yard	1 yard
Backing Fabric	5 yards	5½ yards	7½ yards
Batting	Twin-Size	Full-Size	Full-Size

Web **Extra**

Go to FonsandPorter.com/pixiestickssizes to download Quilt Top Assembly Diagrams and cutting instructions for these size options.

Crazy-Pieced Blocks

Use this quick and easy method to make blocks for *Pixie Sticks* on page 106.

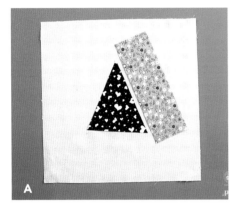
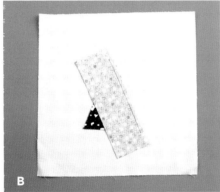

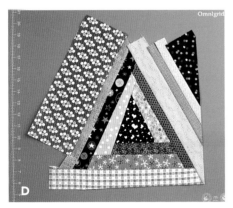

1. Center 1 black print triangle atop 1 muslin foundation square. Cut 1 bright strip longer than side of triangle as shown in *Photo A*.

2. Place strip atop triangle, right sides facing. Stitch through all layers (*Photo B*). Open strip; press.

3. Add bright strips clockwise around center triangle. Fold muslin foundation toward wrong side and trim excess fabric as each strip is added (*Photo C*).

4. Continue adding bright strips until entire foundation square is covered (*Photo D*).

5. Turn unit muslin side up. Trim strips even with edges of muslin square to complete block (*Photos E and F*).

QUILT BY **Karen DuMont**.

MACHINE QUILTED BY **Sara Parrish**.

Traffic Jam

There are no traffic jams on this quilt.

Whimsical vehicles are zipping along on rickrack roads.

PROJECT RATING: EASY

Size: 49" × 47"

MATERIALS

1 yard multicolor stripe for border
and binding

1¼ yards black solid for borders and
wheels

⅞ yard white print

4 fat quarters★ in red, yellow, green,
and black prints for pieced rows

12 (10") squares assorted prints for
vehicles

3¼ yards ½"-wide black rickrack

Paper-backed fusible web

Fons & Porter glue stick (optional)

3 yards backing fabric

Crib-size quilt batting

★fat quarter = 18" × 20"

Cutting

Measurements include ¼" seam
allowances. Border strips are exact
length needed. You may want to make
them longer to allow for piecing
variations. Patterns for appliqué shapes
are on page 116. Follow manufacturer's
instructions for using fusible web. For
step-by-step photos and a video, see
Sew Easy: Fusible Web Apppliqué at
fonsandporter.com/fusiblewebapp.

From multicolor stripe, cut:

• 6 (2½"-wide) strips. Piece strips to
make 4 (2½" × 53½") strips for border.

• 6 (2¼"-wide) strips for binding.

From black solid, cut:

• 6 (4½"-wide) strips. Piece strips to
make 4 (4½" × 53½") strips for border.

• 6 (1½"-wide) strips. Piece strips to
make 4 (1½" × 53½") strips for border.

• 24 Tires.

• 5 Windows.

• 3 Sports Car Rag Tops.

• 1 Sports Car Rag Top reversed.

• 3 Sports Car Windshields.

• 1 Sports Car Windshield reversed.

From white print, cut:

• 3 (8½"-wide) strips. From strips, cut 3
(8½" × 35½") background strips.

From each fat quarter, cut:

• 4 (2"-wide) strips. Cut strips into
random lengths from 3½"–6½".

From 10" squares, cut:

• 2 Trucks.

• 2 Trucks reversed.

• 1 Sedan.

• 3 Sedans reversed.

• 1 Sports Car.

• 3 Sports Cars reversed.

• 4 sets of Sports Car Fenders.

• 2 Windows.

Row Assembly

1. Referring to photo, position rick-rack atop 1 white print background strip. Stitch in place through center of rickrack.

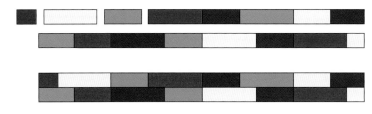

Pieced Row Diagrams

> ### Sew **Smart**™
> Use a dab of glue from glue stick to hold rickrack in place.
> —Marianne

2. Arrange appliqué pieces atop 1 white print background strip; fuse in place. Machine blanket stitch using black thread on print pieces and gray thread on black pieces. Make 3 appliqué rows.

3. Join 1½"-wide strips end to end to make one long strip. From strip, cut 6 (1½" × 35½") sections. Join 2 sections to make 1 pieced row *(Pieced Row Diagrams)*. Make 3 pieced rows.

Quilt Assembly

1. Lay out rows as shown in *Quilt Top Assembly Diagram*. Join rows to complete quilt center.

2. Referring to *Quilt Top Assembly Diagram*, join 1 (1½"-wide) black border strip, 1 stripe border strip, and 1 (4½"-wide) black border strip to make 1 border. Make 4 borders.

3. Add borders to quilt center, mitering corners.

   NOTE: For instructions on mitering borders, see *Sew Easy: Mitered Borders* on page 117.

Quilt Top Assembly Diagram

Finishing

1. Divide backing into 2 (1½-yard) lengths. Cut 1 piece in half length-wise to make 2 narrow panels. Join 1 narrow panel to wider panel. Remaining panel is extra and can be used to make a hanging sleeve.

2. Layer backing, batting, and quilt top; baste. Quilt as desired. Quilt shown was outline quilted around the appliqué and with continuous loops and words "beep beep" in border using variegated thread. *(Quilting Diagram).*

3. Join 2¼"-wide multicolor stripe strips into 1 continuous piece for straight-grain French-fold binding. Add binding to quilt.

DESIGNER

Karen DuMont enjoys designing bright, whimsical appliqué quilts as well as teaching and presenting trunk shows for guilds and shops.

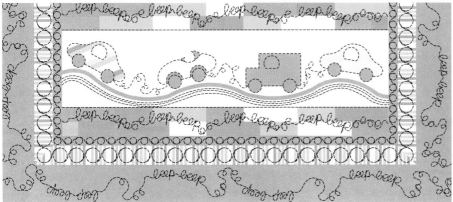

Quilting Diagram

beep beep   beep beep

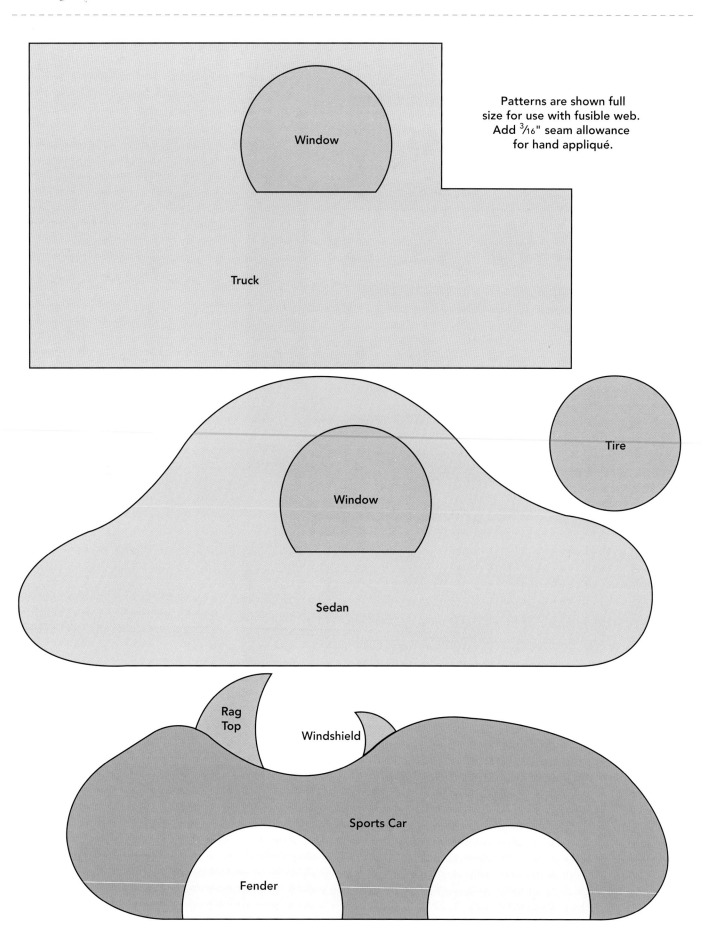

Window

Truck

Patterns are shown full size for use with fusible web. Add $^{3}/_{16}$" seam allowance for hand appliqué.

Tire

Window

Sedan

Rag Top

Windshield

Sports Car

Fender

Sew Easy™ Mitered Borders

The subtle seam of a mitered corner creates the illusion of a continuous line around the quilt. Mitered corners are ideal for striped borders, pieced borders, or multiple plain borders.

1. Referring to *Measuring Quilt Center Diagram*, measure your quilt length through the middle of the quilt rather than along the edges. Then measure quilt width. Add to measurements twice the width of the border plus 2". Trim borders to these measurements.

Measuring Quilt Center Diagram

2. On wrong side of quilt top, mark ¼" seam allowances at each corner.

3. Fold quilt top in half and place a pin at the center of the quilt side. Fold border in half and mark center with pin.

4. With right sides facing and raw edges aligned, match center pins on the border and the quilt. Working from the center out, pin the border to the quilt, right sides facing. The border will extend beyond the quilt edges. Do not trim the border.

5. Sew the border to the quilt. Start and stop stitching ¼" from the corner of the quilt top, backstitching at each end. Press the seam allowance toward the border. Add the remaining borders in the same manner.

6. With right sides facing, fold the quilt diagonally as shown in *Mitering Diagram 1*, aligning the raw edges of the adjacent borders. Pin securely.

7. Align a ruler along the diagonal fold, as shown in *Mitering Diagram 2*. Holding the ruler firmly, mark a line from the end of the border seam to the raw edge.

8. Start machine-stitching at the beginning of the marked line, backstitch, and then stitch on the line out to the raw edge.

9. Unfold the quilt to be sure that the corner lies flat (*Mitered Borders Diagram*). Correct the stitching if necessary. Trim the seam allowance to ¼".

10. Miter the remaining corners. Press the corner seams open.

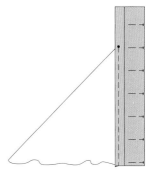

Mitering Diagram 1

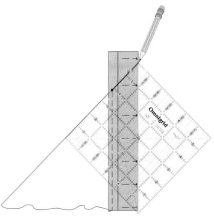

Mitering Diagram 2

Mitered Borders Diagram

Scrap Box Diamonds

This quilt is perfect for those who save even the tiniest scraps of fabric. You know who you are!

PROJECT RATING: INTERMEDIATE

Size: 19" × 26"

MATERIALS

Variety of scraps in assorted prints
½ yard olive print for sashing
1 fat eighth★ dark olive print for
    border corners
⅜ yard cheddar print for border
¼ yard black print for binding
¾ yard muslin for foundation
Spray Starch (optional)
⅝ yard backing fabric
Craft-size quilt batting
★fat eighth = 9" × 20"

Cutting

Measurements include ¼" seam allowances.

From assorted scraps, cut:
- Strips of various widths (1"–2½") and lengths (3"–17").

From olive print, cut:
- 10 (1¼"-wide) strips. From strips, cut 2 (1¼" × 29"), 2 (1¼" × 26"), 2 (1¼" × 19"), 2 (1¼" × 8"), and 30 (1¼" × 4¾") sashing strips.

From dark olive print fat eighth, cut:
- 1 (3"-wide) strip. From strip, cut 4 (3") squares.

From cheddar print, cut:
- 3 (3"-wide) strips.

From black print, cut:
- 3 (2¼"-wide) strips for binding.

From muslin, cut:
- 2 (11"-wide) strips. From strips, cut 5 (11") squares.

Diamond Assembly

1. Referring to *Sew Easy: String Piecing* on page 121, make 5 string pieced squares. Trim strips even with sides of muslin foundation square.

2. With muslin side up, cut from corner to corner of muslin square perpendicular to the stitching lines *(Cutting Diagrams)*.

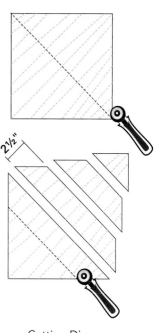

Cutting Diagrams

3. Measuring from this diagonal cut, cut 2½"-wide strips.

4. Referring to *Diamond Cutting Diagrams*, cut 39 (2½"-wide diamonds by placing 2½" line on ruler along angled edge.

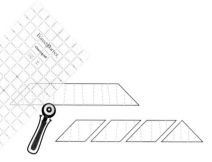

Diamond Cutting Diagrams

Sew Smart™

Spray the muslin side of pieced unit with starch and press before cutting diamonds. —Marianne

Quilt Assembly

1. Lay out diamonds and sashing strips as shown in *Center Diagrams*. Join into diagonal rows; join rows, aligning sashing strips in each row.

2. Draw line on pieced center, placing ¼" line on ruler on the outer-most diamond/sashing connection at top. Cut on drawn line. Repeat for bottom and sides of pieced center.

3. Measure length of quilt. From cheddar print strips, cut 2 side borders that length. Measure width of quilt. From cheddar print strips, cut top and bottom borders that length.

4. Referring to *Quilt Top Assembly Diagram*, add side borders to quilt center.

5. Add 1 dark olive print square to each end of top and bottom borders. Add borders to quilt.

Finishing

1. Layer backing, batting, and quilt top; baste. Quilt as desired. Quilt shown was quilted in the ditch, and with a diamond design in border *(Quilting Diagram)*.

2. Join 2¼"-wide black print strips into 1 continuous piece for straight-grain French-fold binding. Add binding to quilt. ✳

Quilt Top Assembly Diagram

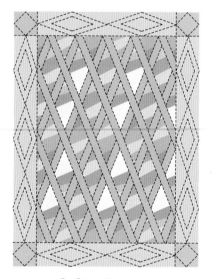

Quilting Diagram

DESIGNER

Annemarie Yohnk, designer for Quilts Remembered, has been quilting since 1980. At home in Burnsville, Minnesota, she is surrounded by antique quilts that serve as her inspiration and a link to the past.

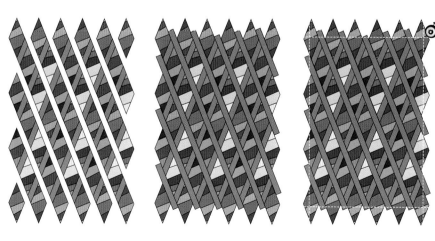

Center Diagrams

String Piecing

This fun patchwork method results in blocks that are each unique.
It's similar to paper foundation piecing, without lines to stitch on.

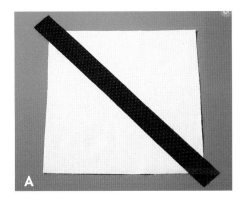
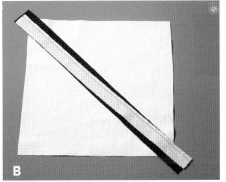

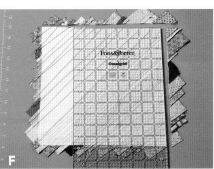

1. Place 1 print strip, right side up from corner to corner, atop 1 muslin square (Photo A).
2. Place second print strip at a slight angle over first strip, with right sides facing. Stitch with ¼" seam allowance along long edge of second strip (Photo B).
3. Trim first strip leaving ¼" beyond stitching (Photo C).

Sew Smart™
Fold the muslin back on itself. Use rotary cutter and ruler to "clean up" the seam allowance edge.
—Liz

4. Press open to reveal second strip (Photo D).

5. Repeat this sew and flip process until the foundation square is covered (Photo E).
6. Trim strips even with edges of muslin square (Photo F).

Monkey Business

Sometimes, less is more. Evelyn Young's quilt is beautiful in its simplicity. The authentic naturally-dyed indigo fabrics from South Africa add to its beauty.

PROJECT RATING: INTERMEDIATE

Size: 54" × 66"

Blocks: 32 (6") Monkey Wrench blocks

MATERIALS

NOTE: Dark fabrics in the quilt shown are Shweshwe prints from South Africa by Marula Imports. Light fabrics are from Marsha McCloskey's Staples collection for Clothworks.

12 fat quarters★★ assorted dark prints

12 fat quarters★ assorted light prints

⅝ yard binding fabric

3½ yards backing fabric

Twin-size quilt batting

★★ Shweshwe fat quarter = 18" × 18"

★fat quarter = 18" × 20"

NOTE: Authentic Shweshwe is 36" wide. It must be washed prior to use to remove excess dye and starch. Refer to Shweshwe Washing Instructions on page 125. Read more about Shweshwe on page 125.

Cutting

Measurements include ¼" seam allowances.

From each dark print fat quarter, cut:

- 2 (6½"-wide) strips. From 1 strip, cut 2 (6½") A squares. From 1 strip, cut 1 (6½") A square and 6 (2⅞") squares. Cut 2⅞" squares in half diagonally to make 12 half-square C triangles.
- 2 (1½"-wide) strips for strip sets.

From each light print fat quarter, cut:

- 2 (6½"-wide) strips. From 1 strip, cut 2 (6½") A squares and 3 (2½") B squares. From 1 strip, cut 1 (6½") A square and 6 (2⅞") squares. Cut 2⅞" squares in half diagonally to make 12 half-square C triangles.
- 2 (1½"-wide) strips for strip sets.

From binding fabric, cut:

- 7 (2¼"-wide) strips for binding.

Block Assembly

1. Join 1 dark print strip and 1 light print strip as shown in *Strip Set Diagram*. Make 2 matching strip sets. From strip sets, cut 12 (2½"-wide) segments.

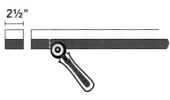

Strip Set Diagram

2. Select 1 matching set of 4 strip set segments, 4 dark print C triangles, 4 light print C triangles, and 1 light print B square.

3. Join 1 light print C triangle and 1 dark print C triangle as shown in *Triangle-Square Diagrams*. Make 4 triangle-squares.

Triangle-Square Diagrams

4. Lay out triangle-squares, strip set segments, and B square as shown in *Block Assembly Diagram*. Join into rows; join rows to complete 1 Monkey Wrench block *(Block Diagram)*. Make 32 Monkey Wrench blocks.

Block Assembly Diagram

Block Diagram

Quilt Assembly

1. Lay out blocks and A squares as shown in *Quilt Top Assembly Diagram*.

2. Join into rows; join rows to complete quilt top.

Finishing

1. Divide backing into 2 (1¾-yard) lengths. Join panels lengthwise. Seam will run horizontally.

2. Layer backing, batting, and quilt top; baste. Quilt as desired. Quilt shown was quilted with a fleur-de-lis design in the blocks and light A squares, and with parallel straight lines in the dark A (border) squares (*Quilting Diagram*).

3. Join 2¼"-wide binding strips into 1 continuous piece for straight-grain French-fold binding. Add binding to quilt.

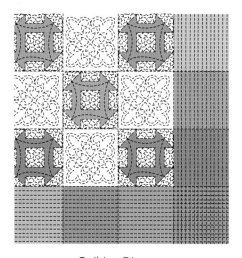

Quilting Diagram

Quilt Top Assembly Diagram

TRIED & TRUE

This block also looks great in bright colors. We used black-and-white and lime green fabrics from Maywood Studios. The collection is called 13 Going on Thirty.

DESIGNER

Evelyn Young is an award-winning quilter and pattern designer who enjoys every part of quilting— from selection of fabrics to the last stitch in the binding. She is inspired by fabric, and loves to use many different prints in her quilts.

Shweshwe Washing Instructions

1. Serge or zigzag fabric edges before washing.
2. Wash in cold water using non-phosphate degergent such as Orvus, Ivory, or Dreft.
3. High water level ensures water will adequately circulate through the fabric.
4. Rinse in cold water. Run fabric through additional rinse cycles until water runs clear.
5. Dry flat or tumble dry. Shweshwe shrinks when machine dried, so be sure to tumble dry for any projects that will be washed later.
6. Press using cotton setting on iron.

About Shweshwe Fabric

Shweshwe is manufactured in South Africa by Da Gama Textiles—the only known producer of traditional indigo-dyed discharge printed fabric in the world. The intricate indigo, white, chocolate brown, and red prints remain in steady demand for traditional African clothing and tourism products, and now for quiltmaking in America.

It is believed by some that the name Shweshwe comes from the swishing sound the fabric makes when the wearer walks. However, according to Da Gama Textiles' history, the cloth was gifted to, and named for, King Moshoeshoe. By association with the king, the cloth was called shoeshoe, and eventually shweshwe.

Shweshwe fabric is 36" wide, and is dyed using natural indigo from many different plants. Indigo itself is not a true dye, but when used, produces a chemical reaction between the fabric and the agent. When fabric is pulled out of the dye pot, the agent oxidizes with air to produce the beautiful blue color.

To read more about Shweshwe, go to marulaimports.danemcoweb.com and indigo.cottoninthecabin.com

SIZE OPTIONS

	Crib (30" × 48")	Full (84" × 96")
Blocks	9	84

MATERIALS

	Crib (30" × 48")	Full (84" × 96")
Dark prints	4 fat quarters★	28 fat quarters★
Light prints	4 fat quarters★	28 fat quarters★
Binding fabric	½ yard	¾ yard
Backing Fabric	1½ yards	7¾ yards
Batting	Crib-size	Queen-size

★ fat quarter = 18" × 20"

Web **Extra**

Go to FonsandPorter.com/mbusisizes to download Quilt Top Assembly Diagrams for these size options.

Dash Around the Square

Debra made this quilt after several block-making sessions with Liz Porter and friends.
They made more than 300 blocks, and then divided them among the group.
Each quilter designed a different setting for her blocks.

PROJECT RATING: INTERMEDIATE

Size: 70" × 70"

Blocks: 121 (5") Churn Dash blocks

MATERIALS

14 fat quarters★ assorted dark prints

14 fat quarters★ assorted light prints

2¾ yards brown print

Fons & Porter Half & Quarter
    Ruler (optional)

4¼ yards backing fabric

Twin-size quilt batting

★fat quarter = 18" × 20"

Cutting

Measurements include ¼" seam allowances. Border strips are exact length needed. Instructions are written for using the Fons & Porter Half & Quarter Ruler. For instructions on using this ruler, go to FonsandPorter.com/chst. If not using this ruler, follow cutting **NOTES**.

From each dark print fat quarter, cut:

• 3 (2½"-wide) strips. From strips, cut 36 half-square triangles.

  NOTE: If not using the Fons and Porter Half & Quarter Ruler, cut 3 (2⅞"-wide) strips. From strips, cut 18 (2⅞") squares. Cut squares in half diagonally to make 36 half-square triangles.

• 3 (1½"-wide) strips. From strips, cut 36 (1½") squares.

From each light print fat quarter, cut:

• 3 (2½"-wide) strips. From strips, cut 36 half-square triangles.

NOTE: If not using the Fons and Porter Half & Quarter Ruler, cut 3 (2⅞"-wide) strips. From strips, cut 18 (2⅞") squares. Cut squares in half diagonally to make 36 half-square triangles.

• 4 (1½"-wide) strips. From strips, cut 45 (1½") squares.

From brown print, cut:

• 8 (2¼"-wide) strips for binding.

From remainder of brown print, cut:

Refer to *Border Cutting Diagram* on page 128.

• 12 (3"-wide) **lengthwise** strips. From strips, cut:

  • 2 (3" × 70½") border J.
  • 2 (3" × 65½") border I.
  • 2 (3" × 55½") border H.
  • 2 (3" × 50½") border G.
  • 2 (3" × 40½") border F.
  • 2 (3" × 35½") border E.
  • 2 (3" × 25½") border D.
  • 2 (3" × 20½") border C.
  • 2 (3" × 10½") border B.
  • 2 (3" × 5½") border A.

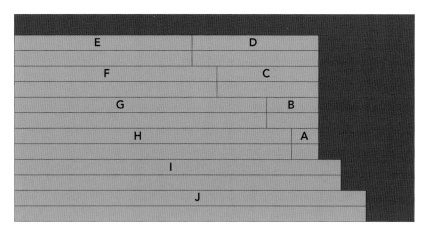

Border Cutting Diagram

Block Assembly

1. Join 1 dark print triangle and 1 light print triangle as shown in *Triangle-Square Diagrams.* Make 4 matching triangle-squares.

Triangle-Square Diagrams

2. Lay out triangle-squares, 4 matching dark print 1½" squares, and 5 matching light print 1½" squares as shown in *Block Assembly Diagram.* Join into rows; join rows to complete 1 block *(Block Diagram).* Make 121 blocks.

Block Assembly Diagram

Block Diagram

Quilt Assembly

1. Lay out 1 block, 2 brown print A borders, and 2 brown print B borders. Join as shown in *Center Unit Diagrams.*

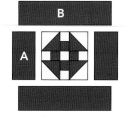

Center Unit Diagrams

2. Join 2 blocks to make 1 side unit *(Side Unit Diagrams).* Make 2 side units. Add to sides of center unit.

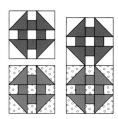

Side Unit Diagrams

3. Join 4 blocks to make top unit *(Top Unit Diagrams).* Repeat for bottom unit. Add to center unit.

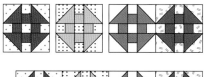

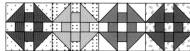

Top Unit Diagrams

4. Referring to *Quilt Top Assembly Diagram,* add brown print borders C and D to quilt.

5. Continue in this manner, adding rows of blocks and brown print borders in alphabetical order to complete quilt top.

Quilt Top Assembly Diagram

Finishing

1. Divide backing into 2 (2⅛-yard) lengths. Cut 1 piece in half length-wise to make 2 narrow panels. Join 1 narrow panel to each side of wider panel; press seam allowances toward narrow panels.

2. Layer backing, batting, and quilt top; baste. Quilt as desired. Quilt shown was quilted with allover meandering *(Quilting Diagram)*.

3. Join 2¼"-wide brown print strips into 1 continuous piece for straight-grain French-fold binding. Add binding to quilt.

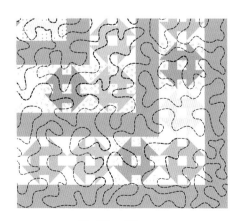

Quilting Diagram

SIZE OPTIONS

	Table Topper (15" × 25")	Twin (70" × 85")
Blocks	8	160

MATERIALS

	Table Topper	Twin
Assorted Dark Prints	8 fat eighths★★	18 fat quarters★
Assorted Light Prints	8 fat eighths★★	18 fat quarters★
Brown Print	⅜ yard	3½ yards
Backing Fabric	⅜ yard	5 yards
Batting	15" × 26" rectangle	Twin-Size

★fat quarter = 18" × 20"

★★fat eighth = 9" × 20"

Web **Extra**

Go to FonsandPorter.com/dasharoundsizes to download Quilt Top Assembly Diagrams and cutting instructions for these size options.

TRIED & TRUE

We made our version with bright prints on a white background for a contemporary look.
Print fabrics are by Moda.

General Instructions

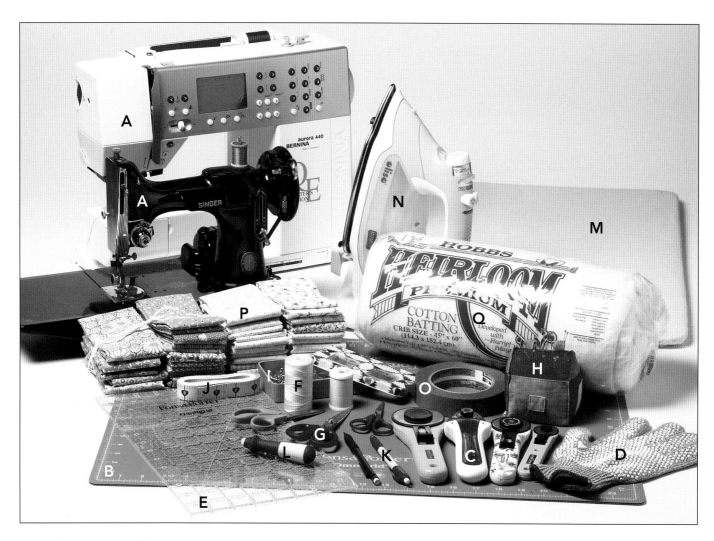

Basic Supplies

You'll need a **sewing machine (A)** in good working order to construct patchwork blocks, join blocks together, add borders, and machine quilt. We encourage you to purchase a machine from a local dealer, who can help you with service in the future, rather than from a discount store. Another option may be to borrow a machine from a friend or family member. If the machine has not been used in a while, have it serviced by a local dealer to make sure it is in good working order. If you need an extension cord, one with a surge protector is a good idea.

A **rotary cutting mat (B)** is essential for accurate and safe rotary cutting. Purchase one that is no smaller than 18" × 24".

Rotary cutting mats are made of "self-healing" material that can be used over and over.

A **rotary cutter (C)** is a cutting tool that looks like a pizza cutter, and has a very sharp blade. We recommend starting with a standard size 45mm rotary cutter. Always lock or close your cutter when it is not in use, and keep it out of the reach of children.

A **safety glove** (also known as a *Klutz Glove*) **(D)** is also recommended. Wear your safety glove on the hand that is holding the ruler in place. Because it is made of cut-resistant material, the safety glove protects your non-cutting hand from accidents that can occur if your cutting hand slips while cutting.

An acrylic **ruler (E)** is used in combination with your cutting mat and rotary cutter. We recommend the Fons & Porter

8" × 14" ruler, but a 6" × 12" ruler is another good option. You'll need a ruler with inch, quarter-inch, and eighth-inch markings that show clearly for ease of measuring. Choose a ruler with 45-degree-angle, 30-degree-angle, and 60-degree-angle lines marked on it as well.

Since you will be using 100% cotton fabric for your quilts, use **cotton or cotton-covered polyester thread (F)** for piecing and quilting. Avoid 100% polyester thread, as it tends to snarl.

Keep a pair of small **scissors (G)** near your sewing machine for cutting threads.

Thin, good quality **straight pins (H)** are preferred by quilters. The pins included with pin cushions are normally too thick to use for piecing, so discard them. Purchase a box of nickel-plated brass **safety pins** size #1 **(I)** to use for pin-basting the layers of your quilt together for machine quilting.

Invest in a 120"-long dressmaker's **measuring tape (J)**. This will come in handy when making borders for your quilt.

A 0.7–0.9mm mechanical **pencil (K)** works well for marking on your fabric.

Invest in a quality sharp **seam ripper (L)**. Every quilter gets well-acquainted with her seam ripper!

Set up an **ironing board (M)** and **iron (N)** in your sewing area. Pressing yardage before cutting, and pressing patchwork seams as you go are both essential for quality quiltmaking. Select an iron that has steam capability.

Masking **tape (O)** or painter's tape works well to mark your sewing machine so you can sew an accurate ¼" seam. You will also use tape to hold your backing fabric taut as you prepare your quilt sandwich for machine quilting.

The most exciting item that you will need for quilting is **fabric (P)**. Quilters generally prefer 100% cotton fabrics for their quilts. This fabric is woven from cotton threads, and has a lengthwise and a crosswise grain. The term "bias" is used to describe the diagonal grain of the fabric. If you make a 45-degree angle cut through a square of cotton fabric, the cut edges will be bias edges, which are quite stretchy. As you learn more quiltmaking techniques, you'll learn how bias can work to your advantage or disadvantage.

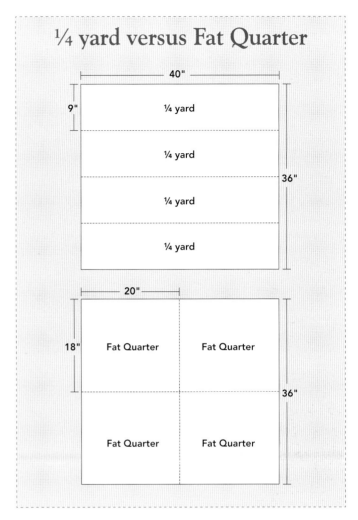

Fabric is sold by the yard at quilt shops and fabric stores. Quilting fabric is generally about 40"–44" wide, so a yard is about 40" wide by 36" long. As you collect fabrics to build your own personal stash, you will buy yards, half yards (about 18" × 40"), quarter yards (about 9" × 40"), as well as other lengths.

Many quilt shops sell "fat quarters," a special cut favored by quilters. A fat quarter is created by cutting a half yard down the fold line into two 18" × 20" pieces (fat quarters) that are sold separately. Quilters like the nearly square shape of the fat quarter because it is more useful than the narrow regular quarter yard cut.

Batting (Q) is the filler between quilt top and backing that makes your quilt a quilt. It can be cotton, polyester, cotton-polyester blend, wool, silk, or other natural materials, such as bamboo or corn. Make sure the batting you buy is at least six inches wider and six inches longer than your quilt top.

Accurate Cutting

Measuring and cutting accuracy are important for successful quilting. Measure at least twice, and cut once!

Cut strips across the fabric width unless directed otherwise.

Cutting for patchwork usually begins with cutting strips, which are then cut into smaller pieces. First, cut straight strips from a fat quarter:

1. Fold fat quarter in half with selvage edge at the top (*Photo A*).

2. Straighten edge of fabric by placing ruler atop fabric, aligning one of the lines on ruler with selvage edge of fabric (*Photo B*). Cut along right edge of ruler.

3. Rotate fabric, and use ruler to measure from cut edge to desired strip width (*Photo C*). Measurements in instructions include ¼" seam allowances.

4. After cutting the required number of strips, cut strips into squares and label them.

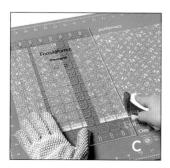

Setting up Your Sewing Machine

Sew Accurate ¼" Seams

Standard seam width for patchwork and quiltmaking is ¼". Some machines come with a patchwork presser foot, also known as a quarter-inch foot. If your machine doesn't have a quarter-inch foot, you may be able to purchase one from a dealer. Or, you can create a quarter-inch seam guide on your machine using masking tape or painter's tape.

Place an acrylic ruler on your sewing machine bed under the presser foot. Slowly turn handwheel until the tip of the needle barely rests atop the ruler's quarter-inch mark (*Photo A*). Make sure the lines on the ruler are parallel to the lines on the machine throat plate. Place tape on the machine bed along edge of ruler (*Photo B*).

Take a Simple Seam Test

Seam accuracy is critical to machine piecing, so take this simple test once you have your quarter-inch presser foot on your machine or have created a tape guide.

Place 2 (2½") squares right sides together, and sew with a scant ¼" seam. Open squares and finger press seam. To finger press, with right sides facing you, press the seam to one side with your fingernail. Measure across pieces, raw edge to raw edge (*Photo C*). If they measure 4½", you have passed the test! Repeat the test as needed to make sure you can confidently sew a perfect ¼" seam.

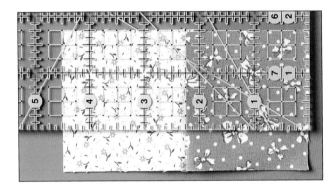

Sewing Comfortably

Other elements that promote pleasant sewing are good lighting, a comfortable chair, background music—and chocolate! Good lighting promotes accurate sewing. The better you can see what you are working on, the better your results. A comfortable chair enables you to sew for longer periods of time. An office chair with a good back rest and adjustable height works well. Music helps keep you relaxed. Chocolate is, for many quilters, simply a necessity.

Tips for Patchwork and Pressing

As you sew more patchwork, you'll develop your own shortcuts and favorite methods. Here are a few favored by many quilters:

- As you join patchwork units to form rows, and join rows to form blocks, press seams in opposite directions from row to row whenever possible (*Photo A*). By pressing seams one direction in the first row and the opposite direction in the next row, you will often create seam allowances that abut when rows are joined (*Photo B*). Abutting or nesting seams are ideal for forming perfectly matched corners on the right side of your quilt blocks and quilt top. Such pressing is not always possible, so don't worry if you end up with seam allowances facing the same direction as you join units.

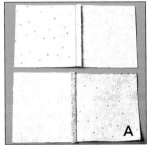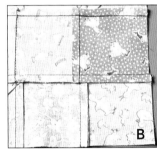

- Sew on and off a small, folded fabric square to prevent bobbin thread from bunching at throat plate (*Photo C*). You'll also save thread, which means fewer stops to wind bobbins, and fewer hanging threads to be snipped. Repeated use of the small piece of fabric gives it lots of thread "legs," so some quilters call it a spider.

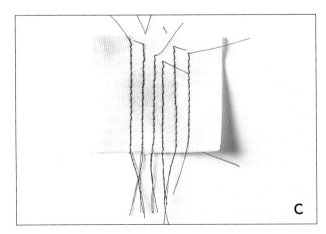

Chain piece patchwork to reduce the amount of thread you use, and minimize the number and length of threads you need to trim from patchwork. Without cutting threads at the end of a seam, take 3–4 stitches without any fabric under the needle, creating a short thread chain approximately ⅛" long (*Photo D*). Repeat until you have a long line of pieces. Remove chain from machine, clip threads between units, and press seams.

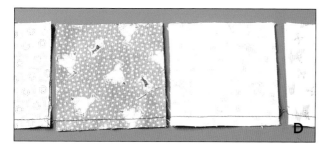

Trim off tiny triangle tips (sometimes called dog ears) created when making triangle-square units (*Photo E*). Trimming triangles reduces bulk and makes patchwork units and blocks lie flatter. Though no one will see the back of your quilt top once it's quilted, a neat back free of dangling threads and patchwork points is the mark of a good quilter. Also, a smooth, flat quilt top is easier to quilt, whether by hand or machine.

Careful pressing will make your patchwork neat and crisp, and will help make your finished quilt top lie flat. Ironing and pressing are two different skills. Iron fabric to remove wrinkles using a back and forth, smoothing motion. Press patchwork and quilt blocks by raising and gently lowering the iron atop your work. After sewing a patchwork unit, first press the seam with the unit closed, pressing to set, or embed, the stitching. Setting the seam this way will help produce straight, crisp seams. Open the unit and press on the right side with the seam toward the darkest

fabric, being careful to not form a pleat in your seam, and carefully pressing the patchwork flat.

Many quilters use finger pressing to open and flatten seams of small units before pressing with an iron. To finger press, open patchwork unit with right side of fabric facing you. Run your fingernail firmly along seam, making sure unit is fully open with no pleat.

Careful use of steam in your iron will make seams and blocks crisp and flat (*Photo F*). Aggressive ironing can stretch blocks out of shape, and is a common pitfall for new quilters.

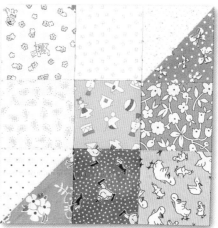

Adding Borders

Follow these simple instructions to make borders that fit perfectly on your quilt.

1. Find the length of your quilt by measuring through the quilt center, not along the edges, since the edges may have stretched. Take 3 measurements and average them to determine the length to cut your side borders (*Diagram A*). Cut 2 side borders this length.

2. Fold border strips in half to find center. Pinch to create crease mark or place a pin at center. Fold quilt top in half crosswise to find center of side. Attach side borders to quilt center by pinning them at the ends and the center, and easing in any fullness. If quilt edge is a bit longer than border, pin and sew with border on top; if border is

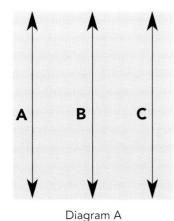

Diagram A

A ————————

B ————————

C ————————

TOTAL ————————

———————— ÷3

AVERAGE
LENGTH ————————

HELPFUL TIP
**Use the following decimal conversions to calculate
your quilt's measurements:**

⅛" = .125	⅝" = .625
¼" = .25	¾" = .75
⅜" = .375	⅞" = .875
½" = .5	

slightly longer than quilt top, pin and sew with border on the bottom. Machine feed dogs will ease in the fullness of the longer piece. Press seams toward borders.

3. Find the width of your quilt by measuring across the quilt and side borders (*Diagram B*). Take 3 measurements and average them to determine the length to cut your top and bottom borders. Cut 2 borders this length.

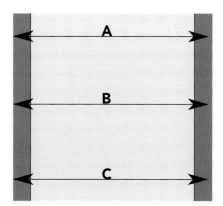

Diagram B

4. Mark centers of borders and top and bottom edges of quilt top. Attach top and bottom borders to quilt, pinnning at ends and center, and easing in any fullness (*Diagram C*). Press seams toward borders.

Diagram C

5. Gently steam press entire quilt top on one side and then the other. When pressing on wrong side, trim off any loose threads.

Joining Border Strips

Not all quilts have borders, but they are a nice complement to a quilt top. If your border is longer than 40", you will need to join 2 or more strips to make a border the required length. You can join border strips with either a straight seam parallel to the ends of the strips (*Photo A* on page 138), or with a diagonal seam. For the diagonal seam method, place one border strip perpendicular to another strip, rights sides facing (*Photo B*). Stitch diagonally across strips as shown. Trim seam allowance to ¼". Press seam open (*Photo C*).

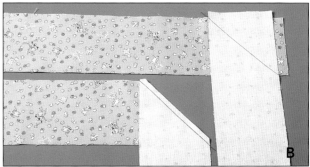

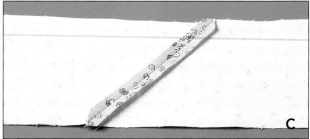

Quilting Your Quilt

Quilters today joke that there are three ways to quilt a quilt—by hand, by machine, or by check. Some enjoy making quilt tops so much, they prefer to hire a professional machine quilter to finish their work. The Split Nine Patch baby quilt shown at left has simple machine quilting that you can do yourself.

Decide what color thread will look best on your quilt top before choosing your backing fabric. A thread color that will blend in with the quilt top is a good choice for beginners. Choose backing fabric that will blend with your thread as well. A print fabric is a good choice for hiding less-than-perfect machine quilting. The backing fabric must be at least 3"–4" larger than your quilt top on all 4 sides. For example: if your quilt top measures 44" × 44", your backing needs to be at least 50" × 50". If your quilt top is 80" × 96", then your backing fabric needs to be at least 86" × 102".

For quilt tops 36" wide or less, use a single width of fabric for the backing. Buy enough length to allow adequate margin at quilt edges, as noted above. When your quilt is wider than 36", one option is to use 60"-, 90"-, or 108"-wide fabric for the quilt backing. Because fabric selection is limited for wide fabrics, quilters generally piece the quilt backing from 44/45"-wide fabric. Plan on 40"–42" of usable fabric width when estimating how much fabric to purchase. Plan your piecing strategy to avoid having a seam along the vertical or horizontal center of the quilt.

For a quilt 37"–60" wide, a backing with horizontal seams is usually the most economical use of fabric. For example, for a quilt 50" × 70", vertical seams would require 152", or 4¼ yards, of 44/45"-wide fabric (76" + 76" = 152"). Horizontal seams would require 112", or 3¼ yards (56" + 56" = 112").

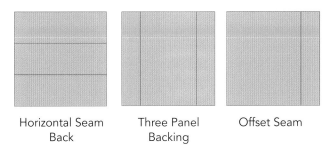

Horizontal Seam Back

Three Panel Backing

Offset Seam

For a quilt 61"–80" wide, most quilters piece a three-panel backing, with vertical seams, from two lengths of fabric. Cut one of the pieces in half lengthwise, and sew the halves to opposite sides of the wider panel. Press the seams away from the center panel.

For a quilt 81"–120" wide, you will need three lengths of fabric, plus extra margin. For example, for a quilt 108" × 108", purchase at least 342", or 9½ yards, of 44/45"-wide fabric (114" + 114" + 114" = 342").

For a three-panel backing, pin the selvage edge of the center panel to the selvage edge of the side panel, with edges aligned and right sides facing. Machine stitch with a ½" seam. Trim seam allowances to ¼", trimming off the selvages from both panels at once. Press the seam away from the center of the quilt. Repeat on other side of center panel.

For a two-panel backing, join panels in the same manner as above, and press the seam to one side.

Create a "quilt sandwich" by layering your backing, batting, and quilt top. Find the crosswise center of the backing fabric by folding it in half. Mark with a pin on each side. Lay backing down on a table or floor, wrong side up. Tape corners and edges of backing to the surface with masking or painter's tape so that backing is taut (*Photo A*).

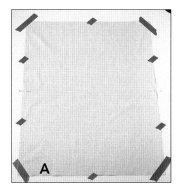

Fold batting in half crosswise and position it atop backing fabric, centering folded edge at center of backing (*Photo B*). Unfold batting and smooth it out atop backing (*Photo C*).

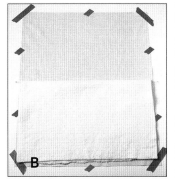
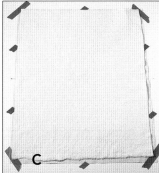

In the same manner, fold the quilt top in half crosswise and center it atop backing and batting (*Photo D*). Unfold top and smooth it out atop batting (*Photo E*).

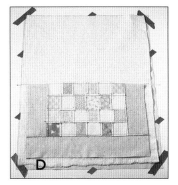
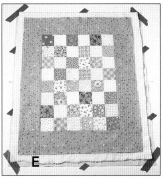

Use safety pins to pin baste the layers (*Photo F*). Pins should be about a fist width apart. A special tool, called a Kwik Klip, or a grapefruit spoon makes closing the pins easier. As you slide a pin through all three layers, slide the point of the pin into one of the tool's grooves. Push on the tool to help close the pin.

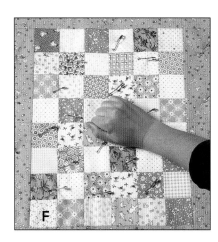

For straight line quilting, install an even feed or walking foot on your machine. This presser foot helps all three layers of your quilt move through the machine evenly without bunching.

Walking Foot   Stitching "in the ditch"

An easy way to quilt your first quilt is to stitch "in the ditch" along seam lines. No marking is needed for this type of quilting.

Binding Your Quilt

Preparing Binding

Strips for quilt binding may be cut either on the straight of grain or on the bias.

1. Measure the perimeter of your quilt and add approximately 24" to allow for mitered corners and finished ends.
2. Cut the number of strips necessary to achieve desired length. We like to cut binding strips 2¼" wide.
3. Join your strips with diagonal seams into 1 continuous piece (*Photo A*). Press the seams open. (See page 142 for instructions for the diagonal seams method of joining strips.)

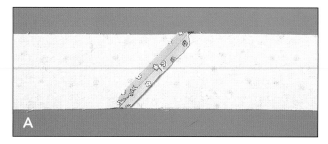

4. Press your binding in half lengthwise, with wrong sides facing, to make French-fold binding (*Photo B*).

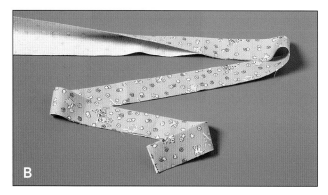

Attaching Binding

Attach the binding to your quilt using an even-feed or walking foot. This prevents puckering when sewing through the three layers.

1. Choose beginning point along one side of quilt. Do not start at a corner. Match the two raw edges of the binding strip to the raw edge of the quilt top. The folded edge

will be free and to left of seam line (*Photo C*). Leave 12" or longer tail of binding strip dangling free from beginning point. Stitch, using ¼" seam, through all layers.

2. For mitered corners, stop stitching ¼" from corner; backstitch, and remove quilt from sewing machine (*Photo D*). Place a pin ¼" from corner to mark where you will stop stitching.

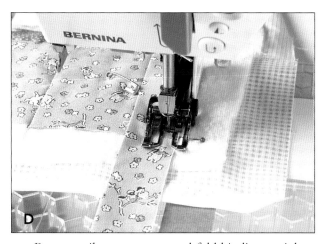

Rotate quilt quarter turn and fold binding straight up, away from corner, forming 45-degree-angle fold (*Photo E*).

Bring binding straight down in line with next edge to be sewn, leaving top fold even with raw edge of previously sewn side (*Photo F*). Begin stitching at top edge, sewing through all layers (*Photo G*).

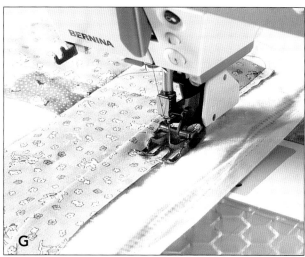

3. To finish binding, stop stitching about 8" away from starting point, leaving about a 12" tail at end (*Photo H*). Bring beginning and end of binding to center of 8" opening and fold each back, leaving about ¼" space

between the two folds of binding (*Photo I*). (Allowing this ¼" extra space is critical, as binding tends to stretch when it is stitched to the quilt. If the folded ends meet at this point, your binding will be too long for the space after the ends are joined.) Crease folds of binding with your fingernail.

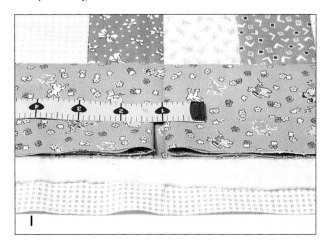

4. Open out each edge of binding and draw line across wrong side of binding on creased fold line, as shown in *Photo J*. Draw line along lengthwise fold of binding at same spot to create an X (*Photo K*).

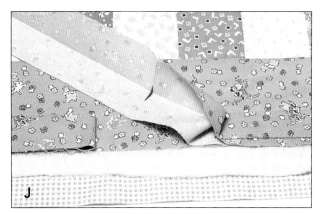

5. With edge of ruler at marked X, line up 45-degree-angle marking on ruler with one long side of binding (*Photo L*). Draw diagonal line across binding as shown in *Photo M*.

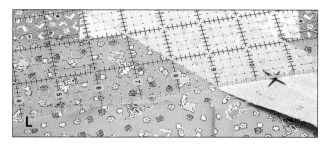

Repeat for other end of binding. Lines must angle in same direction (*Photo N*).

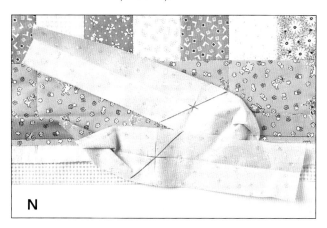

6. Pin binding ends together with right sides facing, pin-matching diagonal lines as shown in *Photo O*. Binding ends will be at right angles to each other. Machine-stitch along diagonal line, removing pins as you stitch (*Photo P*).

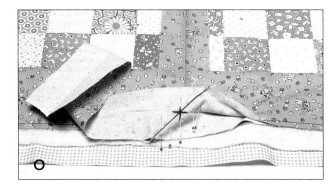

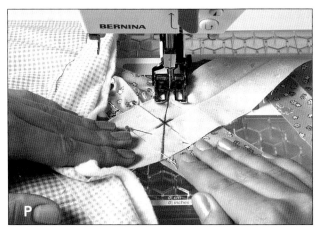

7. Lay binding against quilt to double-check that it is correct length (*Photo Q*). Trim ends of binding ¼" from diagonal seam (*Photo R*).

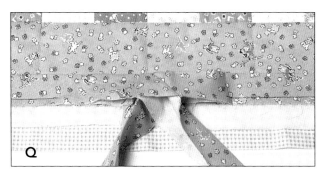

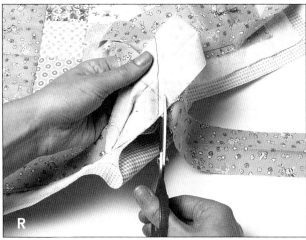

8. Finger press diagonal seam open (*Photo S*). Fold binding in half and finish stitching binding to quilt (*Photo T*).

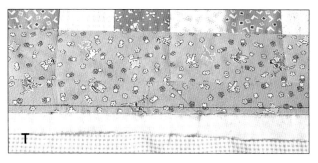

Hand Stitching Binding to Quilt Back

1. Trim any excess batting and quilt back with scissors or a rotary cutter (*Photo A*). Leave enough batting (about ⅛" beyond quilt top) to fill binding uniformly when it is turned to quilt back.

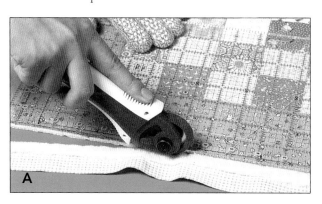

2. Bring folded edge of binding to quilt back so that it covers machine stitching. Blindstitch folded edge to quilt backing, using a few pins just ahead of stitching to hold binding in place (*Photo B*).

3. Continue stitching to corner. Fold unstitched binding from next side under, forming a 45-degree angle and a mitered corner. Stitch mitered folds on both front and back (*Photo C*).

Finishing Touches

● **Label your quilt so the recipient and future generations know who made it.** To make a label, use a fabric marking pen to write the details on a small piece of solid color fabric (*Photo A*). To make writing easier, put pieces of masking tape on the wrong side. Remove tape after writing. Use your iron to turn under ¼" on each edge, then stitch the label to the back of your quilt using a blindstitch, taking care not to sew through to quilt top.

● **Take a photo of your quilt.** Keep your photos in an album or journal along with notes, fabric swatches, and other information about the quilts.

● **If your quilt is a gift, include care instructions.** Some quilt shops carry pre-printed care labels you can sew onto the quilt (*Photo B*). Or, make a care label using the method described above.